the really hungry
VEGAN STUDENT COOKBOOK

the really hungry
VEGAN STUDENT COOKBOOK

OVER 65 PLANT-BASED RECIPES
FOR EATING WELL ON A BUDGET

RYLAND PETERS & SMALL
LONDON • NEW YORK

Senior Designer Toni Kay
Editor Sarah Vaughan
Production Controller
  Mai-ling Collyer
Art Director Leslie Harrington
Editorial Director Julia Charles
Publisher Cindy Richards
Indexer Vanessa Bird

First published in 2020
by Ryland Peters & Small
20–21 Jockey's Fields
London WC1R 4BW
and
341 E 116th St
New York, NY 10029
www.rylandpeters.com

Recipe collection compiled
by Sarah Vaughan.
Text © Nadia Arumugan,
Jordan Bourke, Chloe Coker,
Amy Ruth Finegold, Liz Franklin,
Nicola Graimes, Dunja Gulin,
Vicky Jones, Kathy Kordalis, Anya
Ladra, Jenny Linford, Dan May,
Hannah Miles, Jane Montgomery,
Adriano di Petrillo, Louise
Pickford, Rosa Rigby, Shelagh
Ryan, Jenny Tschiesche, Leah
Vanderveldt, Laura Washburn
Hutton, Jenna Zoe 2020

Design and photographs ©
Ryland Peters & Small 2020

ISBN: 978-1-78879-285-1

10 9 8 7 6 5 4 3 2 1

A CIP record for this book is
available from the British Library.

US Library of Congress
Cataloging-in-Publication data
has been applied for.

Printed and bound in China

NOTES:
◼ Both British (Metric) and
American (Imperial plus
US cup) are included in these
recipes, however it is important
to work with one set of
measurements and not alternate
between the two within a recipe.
◼ All spoon measurements are
level, unless otherwise specified.
◼ Ovens should be preheated to
the specified temperature. If
using a fan-assisted oven, follow
the manufacturer's instructions
for adjusting temperatures.
◼ To sterilize preserving jars,
wash them in hot, soapy water
and rinse in boiling water. Place
in a large saucepan or pot and
cover with hot water. With the
saucepan lid on, bring the water
to a boil and continue boiling for
15 minutes. Turn off the heat
and leave the jars in the hot water
until just before they are to be
filled. Invert the jars onto a clean
dish towel to dry. Sterilize the lids
for 5 minutes, by boiling or
according to the manufacturer's
instructions. Jars should be filled
and sealed while they are still hot.
◼ When a recipe calls for the
grated zest of citrus fruit, buy
unwaxed fruit and wash well
before using. If you can only find
treated fruit, scrub well in warm
soapy water before using.
◼ Always check the product
packaging to ensure the
particular brand of ingredient
you are buying is vegan.

CONTENTS

INTRODUCTION

If you're living away from home for the first time, you're going to need to learn how to cook up a storm in the kitchen and this book is here to show you how. Whether you want to make a stack of pancakes on a lazy Sunday morning, a warming bean stew to fight off those homesick blues or some tasty snacks for your movie night (or to keep you going through the student day!), this book has all you need. It will banish any fears you might have if you're new to cooking, and if you're already getting A grades in culinary arts, you're sure to find some fresh inspiration here. All the recipes are exciting, delicious and 100% vegan! Some are super-quick, while others need a little bit more time, but are definitely worth the wait. Either way, this collection of stress-free recipes won't leave you feeling hungry and will be cheaper and healthier than living on take-out or home deliveries. Check out all the hot tips in Kitchen Know-how on the following pages before you get started – they will make life a whole lot easier and ensure that you can always whip up something tasty, even with just a few good ingredients.

KITCHEN KNOW-HOW

The recipes in this book need the minimum of kitchen equipment. Some recipes will require extras, e.g. a food processor or blender (which can be bought very cheaply), or a baking pan for brownies, etc. but you can go a long way with these essential items:

CHECK LIST

HANDY INGREDIENTS

KITCHEN KIT

★ 2 or 3 sharp knives, including a serrated knife
☑ wooden spoon
★ potato masher
☑ garlic crusher
★ pepper mill
☑ can opener
★ vegetable peeler
☑ 2 chopping boards
★ large mixing bowl
☑ sieve/strainer
★ colander
☑ 1 large and 1 medium saucepan
★ frying pan/skillet with a lid
☑ baking sheet
★ roasting pan

☑ ovenproof dish (Pyrex or ceramic)
★ measuring jug/pitcher
☑ weighing scales/measuring spoons and cups
★ a selection of airtight containers
☑ kettle
★ toaster
☑ kitchen foil
★ clingfilm/plastic wrap
☑ greaseproof paper
★ kitchen paper/paper towels
☑ cleaning stuff, including washing up liquid, sponges and multi-surface cleaner
★ dish towels
☑ oven gloves

★ sea salt
☑ black peppercorns
★ olive oil
☑ vegetable or sunflower oil
★ balsamic vinegar
☑ red or white wine vinegar
★ dark or light soy sauce
☑ tomato ketchup
★ mustard
☑ marmite
★ vegan mayonnaise (or make your own, see page 20)
☑ long-grain rice
★ risotto rice
☑ dried pasta and noodles, including spaghetti

★ couscous
☑ stock cubes or bouillon powder
★ canned chopped tomatoes
☑ a selection of canned beans and legumes, such as kidney beans, chickpeas and lentils
★ a selection of dried and jarred vegetables such as sun-dried tomatoes, olives and capers
☑ a selection of nuts and seeds, such as almonds, cashews, chia seeds and sunflower seeds
★ plain/all-purpose flour
☑ self-raising/rising flour
★ sugar
☑ tomato purée/paste
★ vegan margarine

☑ a selection of dried herbs, such as basil, oregano, rosemary and thyme
★ a selection of dried spices, such as curry powder, ground cumin, ground cinnamon, paprika, chilli/chili powder or chilli flakes/hot red pepper flakes
☑ maple and agave syrups or molasses
★ plant-based milks (or make your own, see page 15)
☑ nut and seed butters (or make your own, see page 16)
★ onions
☑ garlic
★ tofu

FOOD SAFETY

■ Always keep your kitchen clean! Keep it tidy and disinfect work surfaces after use with a mild detergent or an antibacterial cleaner. Keep pets off surfaces and, as far as possible, keep them out of the kitchen.

■ Store food safely to avoid cross-contamination. Keep food in clean, dry, airtight containers, always store raw and cooked foods separately and wash utensils (and your hands) between preparing raw and cooked foods.

■ Wash your hands with hot, soapy water before and after handling food.

■ Never put hot food into a fridge or freezer, as this will increase the internal temperature to an unsafe level and may cause other foods to spoil. Cool leftover food quickly to room temperature, ideally by transferring it to a cold dish, then refrigerate or freeze. Cool large dishes such as stews by putting the dish in a sink of cold water. Stir occasionally then refrigerate once cool. During cooling, cover the food loosely with clingfilm/plastic wrap to protect it.

■ Don't use perishable food beyond the 'use-by' date as it could be a health risk. If you have any doubts about the food, discard it.

■ Reheated food must be piping hot throughout before consumption. Never reheat any type of food more than once.

■ If you are going to freeze food, freeze food that is in prime condition, on the day of purchase, or as soon as a dish is made and cooled. Freeze it quickly and in small quantities, if possible. Label and date food and keep plenty of supplies in the freezer. Always leave a gap in the container when freezing liquids, so that there is enough room for the liquid to expand as it freezes.

■ Use proper oven gloves to remove hot dishes from the oven – don't just use a kitchen towel because you risk burning yourself. Kitchen towels are also a breeding ground for germs, so only use them for drying, and wash them often.

■ Leftover canned foods should be transferred to an airtight container, kept in the fridge and eaten within 2 days. Once cans are opened, the contents should be treated as fresh food.

■ The natural oils in chillies/chiles may cause irritation to your skin and eyes. When preparing them, wear disposable gloves or pull a small plastic bag over each hand, secured with an elastic band around the wrist, to create a glove.

■ Cooked rice is a potential source of food poisoning. Cool leftovers quickly, then store in an airtight container in the fridge and use within 24 hours. Always reheat cooked cold rice to piping hot.

INGREDIENTS TIPS

▪ When substituting dried herbs for fresh, use roughly half the quantity the recipe calls for, as dried herbs have a more concentrated flavour.

▪ Chop leftover fresh herbs, spoon them into an ice-cube tray, top each portion with a little water and freeze. Once solid, put the cubes in a freezer bag. Seal, label and return to the freezer. Add the frozen herb cubes to soups, casseroles and sauces.

▪ The colour of a fresh chilli/chile is no indication of how hot it will be. Generally speaking, the smaller and thinner the chilli/chile, the hotter it will be.

▪ To reduce the heat of a fresh chilli, cut it in half lengthways, then scrape out and discard the seeds and membranes (or core). See also 'food safety' for advice on handling chillies/chiles (see page 9).

▪ Most vegetables keep best in the fridge, but a cool, dark place is also good if you lack fridge space. Potatoes should always be stored in the dark to avoid sprouting, making them inedible.

▪ To skin a tomato, score a cross in its base using a sharp knife. Put them in a heatproof bowl, cover with boiling water, leave for about 30 seconds, then transfer them to a bowl of cold water. When cooled, drain and peel off the skins with a knife.

▪ To clean leeks, trim them, then slit them lengthways about a third of the way through. Open the leaves a little and wash away any dirt from between the layers under cold running water.

▪ Store flour in its original sealed packaging or in an airtight container in a cool, dry, airy place. Buy small quantities at a time to help avoid infestation of psocids (very small, barely visible, grey-brown insects), which may appear even in the cleanest of homes. If you do find these small insects in your flour, dispose of it immediately and wash and dry the container thoroughly. Never mix new flour with old.

▪ If you run out of self-raising/self-rising flour, sift together 2 teaspoons of baking powder with every 225 g/scant 2 cups plain/all-purpose flour. This will not be quite as effective, but it is a good substitute.

▪ Store oils, well sealed, in a cool, dark, dry place, away from direct sunlight. They can be kept in the fridge, but oils such as olive oil tend to solidify and go cloudy in the fridge. If this happens, bring the oil back to room temperature before use.

▪ Small pasta tubes and twists, such as penne and fusilli, are good for chunky vegetable sauces.

▪ Dried pasta has a long shelf life. Store it in its unopened packet or in an airtight container in a cool, dry place. Leftover cooked pasta should be kept in a sealed container in the fridge and used within 2 days. Ordinary cooked pasta does not freeze well on its own, but it will freeze in dishes such as lasagne. Allow 85–115 g/3–4 oz. of dried pasta per person.

▪ Pasta must be cooked in a large volume of salted, boiling water. Once you have added the pasta to the boiling water, give it a stir, then cover the pan to help the water return to a rolling boil as quickly as possible. Remove the lid once the water has started boiling again (to prevent the water boiling over), and stir occasionally. Check the packet instructions for cooking times. When it is ready, cooked pasta should be al dente – tender but with a slight resistance.

▪ Rice may be rinsed before cooking to remove tiny pieces of grit or excess starch. Most packaged rice is checked and clean, however, so rinsing it is unnecessary and will wash away nutrients. Risotto rice is not washed before use – rinse it under cold water until the water runs clear.

▪ As an accompaniment, allow 55–85 g/¼–⅓ cup uncooked rice per person, or for a main like risotto, up to 115 g/½ cup.

▪ Before frying tofu, remove it from its packaging and wrap in kitchen paper/paper towels and press with weight, to remove excess moisture. The drier you get the tofu, the crispier it will be.

KITCHEN WISDOM

▪ To remove odours from a container that you want to use again, fill the container with hot water, then stir in 1 tablespoon baking powder. Leave it to stand overnight, then wash, rinse well and dry before use.

▪ If you transfer foods from packages to storage containers, tape the food label onto the container so you can easily identify its contents and you have a record of the manufacturer's cooking instructions, if necessary. Make a note of the 'best-before' or 'use-by' date on the container, too.

▪ Choose stackable containers to maximize storage space. Remember that square or rectangular containers make better use of shelf space than round or oval containers.

▪ For convenient single servings, freeze portions of home-made soup in large, thick paper cups or small individual containers. Remove them from the freezer as required, defrost and reheat the soup thoroughly before serving.

▪ To make salad dressings or vinaigrettes, put all the ingredients in a clean screw-top jar, seal and shake well. Alternatively, put the ingredients straight into the salad bowl and whisk together well, before adding the salad.

▪ Spirits with an alcohol content of 35% or over can be kept in the freezer – this is ideal for those which should be served ice-cold.

▪ If you are short of space in the kitchen, cover the sink with a piece of wood cut to size or a large chopping board to create an extra work surface when the sink is not in use.

MICROWAVE SAFETY

▪ The more food you are cooking, and the colder it is, the longer it will take to cook in a microwave.

▪ Many foods need to be covered during microwaving. Use microwave-safe clingfilm/plastic wrap, a plate or a lid. Pierce clingfilm/plastic wrap, or leave a gap at one side if using a plate or lid, to allow excess steam to escape.

▪ Never operate a microwave when it is empty, as the microwaves will bounce back to and damage the oven components.

▪ Be careful when stirring heated liquids in a container in the microwave, as they can bubble up without warning.

▪ After food has been removed from the microwave, it will continue to cook due to the residual heat within the food, so adhere to standing times when they are given in recipes.

▪ Use a microwave with a built-in turntable if possible, and make sure that you turn or stir the food several times during cooking to ensure even cooking throughout. The food towards the outer edges usually cooks first.

▪ Metal containers, china with a metallic trim, foil or crystal glass (which contains lead) should not be used in a microwave. Metal reflects microwaves and may damage the oven components. Microwave-safe plastic containers, ovenproof glass and ceramic dishes are all suitable, as is most household glazed china. Paper plates and kitchen paper/paper towels can be used to reheat food for short periods.

VEGAN KNOW-HOW

The choice to follow a vegan diet, or to cut down on the amount of animal-based products we eat, is done for many reasons: ethical, environmental, religious, health, financial or simply personal choice. A basic vegan diet is free from all animal products, including eggs, dairy and even honey. It is important that when food groups are removed from a diet, the balance of key dietary components are reviewed and maintained.

KEY NUTRIENTS IN THE VEGAN DIET

★ **carbohydrates and fibre/fiber** are usually plentiful in a good vegan diet – eating a variety of vegatables and fruit (including skins where possible), potatoes, bran and wholegrains should provide what's needed.

★ **protein** is essential in any diet. It is necessary to the body for growth and repair and the production of enzymes and hormones, and also makes you feel full. An average person should eat around 45–55 g/ 1½–2 oz. of protein a day. In meat-free diets it can be harder to find complete sources of protein. This can be combatted by ensuring that you eat a variety of foods and by mixing different sources of protein in one dish, such as grains with pulses, nuts or seeds. Whilst soya/soy is an excellent source of protein, it can be over-used. Try using a variety of lentils, beans, chickpeas and wholegrains in your cooking. Quinoa is a good source of protein to use in salads or as a substitute for rice. A sprinkling of chopped nuts or seeds is a great way to add extra protein to any meal.

★ **key vitamins and minerals** can sometimes be lacking in vegan diets. As well as what you eat, think about the cooking process – try to eat a substantial and broad range of raw vegetables, or steam and blanch foods to retain as much goodness as possible.

As well as in fruit and vegetables, a lot of essential vitamins can be found in fortified foods such as breakfast cereals and soya/soy milk – these are a good sources of vitamins, as are green vegetables. Vitamin C, found in citrus fruit, is usually plentiful in vegan diets. Not only is it important for the body, it also helps to release minerals from pulses and vegetables, and helps the body to absorb iron – try squeezing some lemon juice over a salad or into a dressing. Vitamin B12 might be the only nutrient for which vegans are strongly advised to take a regular food supplement. If you cut out dairy entirely, it is worth checking your vitamin B12 levels and seeking medical advice on supplements. Whole foods and a versatile vegan diet will give you plenty of nutrients, and if you have a healthy lifestyle, you probably won't need to take any other supplements on a daily basis.

★ **calcium**, for those omitting dairy, can be sourced by eating plenty of leafy green vegetables, sesame seeds, beans and nuts in their diet. Calcium can also be found in soya/soy milk and fortified fruit juices.

★ **iron** intake can be a concern when choosing to follow a meat-free diet, but eating a combination of leafy green vegetables, dried fruits, beans, nuts, seeds and tofu should combat this. However, it may be worth getting medical advice on if you need to take an iron supplement.

★ **fatty acids** are an key part of any diet. Vegan diets are generally low in saturated (bad) fat. Soya/soy, walnuts and seeds are excellent sources of good fats, such as monounsaturated or plant-based omega-3s. Why not try using different oils – linseed, rapeseed and nut oils can be used for cooking and flavouring.

BACK TO BASICS

Home-made nut milks are easy to make. This almond nut milk is great, but you could try cashew, hazelnut, pistachio, peanut, walnut, Brazil or macadamia. Sunflower or pumpkin seed milks are also an option, as is oat milk. Simply follow this recipe with your chosen ingredient!

make-your-own
NUT MILKS

Put the almonds in a large bowl and cover with about 2.5 cm/ 1 inch of pure or filtered water. Cover with a plate and leave to stand overnight. The next day, drain the almonds and rinse them under cold running water.

Put the soaked almonds in a blender with the 750 ml/3 cups of pure or filtered water and blend on a high speed for about 2 minutes, or until the nuts are broken down into a fine meal and the water is creamy white.

Strain the almonds through a nut milk bag or a muslin-lined/ cheesecloth-lined sieve/strainer, reserving the strained milky liquid in a bowl. Gather up the sides of the bag or the muslin/cloth in the sieve/strainer and squeeze to extract as much liquid as possible into the bowl containing the milky liquid. Pour the milk into a lidded container or bottle and store in the fridge for up to 3 days. To be extra savvy, use the nut meal left in the bag or muslin/cloth to blend in smoothies or to make granola, muesli or cookies.

Note This recipe uses three times the quantity of water to nuts for an everyday but still rich milk, but you can reduce the quantity of water to make a thicker milk or even a cream substitute. If you regularly make nut milks, it is worth making a small investment in a nut milk bag, which makes straining and draining the nuts from the milk that much easier.

150 g/generous 1 cup shelled almonds

750 ml/3 cups pure or filtered water, plus extra for soaking

dates, agave or pure maple syrup, to sweeten (optional)

a sprinkling of ground cinnamon or nutmeg, to taste (optional)

MAKES ABOUT 800 ML/3½ CUPS

What vegan diet is complete without nut and seed butters? A few nuts make a good snack, but why not make them more exciting and transform them into a smooth, creamy paste, perfect spread on fruit – and they're full of good fats!

NUT & SEED BUTTERS

For each recipe, place the nuts and seeds in a food processor fitted with an 'S' blade first; initially they will turn into a thick powder, then their natural oils will come through and you'll start to see a 'butter' form. Add the remaining ingredients and pulse until creamy and smooth.

EACH RECIPE MAKES ABOUT 8 SERVINGS (about 2 tablespoons per serving)

BASIC ALMOND BUTTER

170 g/1¼ cup almonds

2 teaspoons pure maple syrup

a pinch of sea salt

This oh-so-simple and basic nut butter will probably always be a favourite because of its sheer versatility. Beyond pairing it with dairy-free yoghurt or fruit, you can drizzle it on porridge or oatmeal, top a baked sweet potato with 1–2 tablespoons' worth, or mix it with some soy sauce and lemon for a great stir-fry base.

WARMING MACA, CINNAMON & HEMP-SEED ALMOND BUTTER

125 g/scant 1 cup almonds

40 g/¼ cup shelled hemp seeds

½ tablespoon ground cinnamon

1 tablespoon maca powder (optional)

½ teaspoon pure vanilla extract

1 teaspoon sugar

2 tablespoons hemp oil (use flaxseed/linseed, coconut or chia oil if you can't find hemp oil)

This is an almond butter variation that can be especially enjoyed in the winter because the cinnamon and maca are very warming to the body. You can also add a big dose of hemp seeds for their amazing omega-3 levels. Pair this with whatever you like, but you can quite easily dunk a big spoon into the jar and eat it straight up.

SPICY SESAME BUTTER

120 g/1 cup sesame seeds

2 tablespoons ground flaxseeds/linseeds

2 tablespoons sesame oil or olive oil

1 tablespoon freshly squeezed lemon juice or apple cider vinegar

1 tablespoon nutritional yeast (optional)

¼ teaspoon sea salt

½–1 teaspoon cayenne pepper

There are many sweet or plain nut butters, but here's a savoury option for when that salty/fatty craving strikes. Spread this on cucumber slices or a cracker. You could even mix it into cooked vegetables, such as green French beans, spinach and red (bell) peppers.

MAPLE & LEMON PUMPKIN-SEED BUTTER

130 g/1 cup pumpkin seeds

1 tablespoon coconut oil

60 ml/¼ cup pure maple syrup

a pinch of sea salt

1 teaspoon freshly squeezed lemon juice

½ teaspoon pure vanilla extract

This sweet and tangy nut butter is perfect to spread on sour green apples. If you're worried about start-of-term coughs and colds, zinc is amazing for giving our immune systems a boost, which the pumpkin seeds in this recipe are full of. This butter is a delicious and painless way to up your levels.

Traditionally, pesto is made with basil, pine nuts and Parmesan. This cheese-free version is made with a mixture of herbs and almonds in place of pine nuts. The zingy flavours make it taste more Asian than Italian, and if you can't find kaffir lime, use lemongrass as a substitute.

ZESTY ALMOND PESTO

Put all the ingredients in a food processor and blitz until they turn into a paste. Store in an airtight container in the fridge for up to 4 days. Pour more olive oil onto the pesto to preserve its bright green colour, if you like.

20 g/1 cup each spinach, mint, parsley and coriander/cilantro, tightly packed

30 g/¼ cup blanched almonds

6 tablespoons extra-virgin olive oil, plus extra to preserve

1 kaffir lime leaf

freshly squeezed juice of 1 lime

grated zest of 1 lemon

1 garlic clove

a pinch of sea salt

EACH RECIPE MAKES ABOUT 200 G/1 CUP

Although traditional guacamole is made with all-healthful ingredients, this version has been lightened up by including a hefty dose of fresh peas and extra veggies, which allow the guacamole to keep its creamy texture and body, but which mellow out the density of the avocado.

LIGHTER GUACAMOLE

Put all the ingredients in a food processor and blitz until smooth. Serve immediately or, if keeping in the fridge, squeeze more lemon juice onto the surface of the dip to prevent the avocado from browning.

1 large avocado, pitted

90 g/1½ cups peas, ideally fresh, but frozen and thawed is fine too

½ red (bell) pepper, deseeded

2 tomatoes

¼ small onion

1 garlic clove

a large handful of fresh coriander/cilantro

freshly squeezed juice of ½ lime

1 tablespoon freshly squeezed lemon juice, plus extra to preserve

If you love creamy sauces, but are avoiding dairy and soy, then here's a great alternative! Cashews are mild in taste and can be used as a base in many delicious recipes, especially those mimicking yoghurt or cream cheese dishes.

CASHEW 'YOGHURT' SAUCE

180 g/1⅓ cups cashews

4 tablespoons freshly squeezed lemon juice, or to taste

1 teaspoon agave syrup (optional)

Put the cashews in a bowl, cover with water and let soak for 24 hours. Drain, discarding the soaking water and rinse well.

Blend the soaked cashews with the rest of the ingredients and 175 ml/¾ cup cold water in a high-speed blender until silky smooth. Keep refrigerated and use within 2 days.

MAKES ABOUT 400 ML/1⅔ CUPS

A vegan version of popular mayonnaise that is much lighter and much less oily than regular mayo, or even the store-bought vegan mayo. This pairs up very well with falafel.

TOFU MAYONNAISE

MAKES ABOUT 240 ML/1 CUP

300 g/2 cups fresh tofu

60 ml/¼ cup olive or sunflower oil

3 tablespoons freshly squeezed lemon juice or apple cider vinegar

1 soft date

½ teaspoon sea salt

Blend all the ingredients together with 6 tablespoons water until completely smooth.

Taste and adjust the seasonings. If you like it tangier you can always add a little more lemon juice or vinegar. Also, pay attention to what you will serve it with; if used as a salad dressing, it needs to be more sour, and if used with salty foods like falafel, make it less salty.

Plastic tubs of coleslaw are really no match for the real thing, and if you like it but have never made it yourself, you simply must. This recipe has a light creamy dressing and derives its sweetness from the apple, which makes for a delicious and healthy change.

APPLE COLESLAW

Put the red cabbage in a heatproof bowl. Heat the wine vinegar in a small saucepan until just boiling. Stir in the salt, then pour the mixture over the red cabbage. Toss well. This helps to set the colour.

In a serving bowl, combine the red cabbage, white cabbage, carrot and apple, and toss well to combine.

To prepare the dressing, put the orange juice, vinegar, salt and sugar in a small bowl and use a fork or small whisk to mix. Add the oil, yoghurt and crème fraîche. Mix well and season to taste with pepper.

Pour the dressing over the cabbage mixture and toss well. Taste for seasoning and adjust if necessary – it may need more salt or more vinegar. Refrigerate for several hours before serving. When ready to serve, sprinkle with toasted pumpkin seeds. This is best eaten on the day it is prepared.

SERVES 6–8

500 g/1 lb. 2 oz. red cabbage (about ½ a cabbage), thinly sliced

3 tablespoons red or white wine vinegar or raspberry vinegar

¼ teaspoon fine sea salt

500 g/1 lb. 2 oz. white cabbage (about ½ a cabbage), thinly sliced

125 g/1 cup grated carrot

1 large tart apple, such as Granny Smith, peeled, cored and coarsely grated

75 g/½ cup pumpkin seeds, toasted

For the dressing

freshly squeezed juice of ½ orange

1 tablespoon cider vinegar

½ teaspoon fine sea salt

1 teaspoon sugar

1 tablespoon vegetable oil

180 g/¾ cup vegan yoghurt

180 g/¾ cup vegan crème fraîche or sour cream

freshly ground black pepper

These make a fantastic topping to a meal or salad. They work really well with many of the Asian-inspired dishes in this book.

CUMIN-ROASTED CHICKPEAS

400-g/14-oz. can chickpeas, drained and rinsed

1 teaspoon garlic powder

1 teaspoon onion powder

½ teaspoon ground cumin

1 tablespoon olive oil

¼–½ teaspoon sea salt

Preheat the oven to 200°C (400°F) Gas 6.

In a bowl, toss the chickpeas in the garlic powder, onion powder, cumin and olive oil.

Put the chickpeas on a sheet pan with sides. Bake in the preheated oven for 30 minutes until lightly toasted. Shake the pan a couple of times during the baking time to ensure the chickpeas cook evenly.

Remove from the oven. Sprinkle over the salt to taste. Serve hot or cold. If serving cold, let cool, then store in an airtight container until ready to be consumed. They are best eaten within 24 hours.

SERVES 2 AS A SIDE DISH

MAKES
48 CUBES

To make stews, ragouts, sauces, curries and other lovely dishes extra yummy, it is very important to marinate and fry the tofu, seitan and tempeh in advance. This way, each piece soaks up spices and forms a nice crunchy crust. In the marinade below, you can adjust the spices, herbs and oils to suit your liking.

PREPARING TOFU, seitan & tempeh

Place the tofu, seitan or tempeh cubes in a deep plate. Put all ingredients for the marinade in a small jar with 2 teaspoons water, close and shake.

Pour this mixture over the cubes and mix well cover all the pieces in the marinade. If the marinade is overly thick, add 1–2 teaspoons of extra water, just to make it runny enough to cover all the cubes. Cover with clingfilm/plastic wrap and let it sit at room temperature for at least 30 minutes. You can also do this a day in advance and let it sit in the fridge.

Put a little flour in a bowl and roll each cube in it until each side is coated in a thin layer, but be careful not to wipe the marinade off. Remove any excess flour by shaking each cube between the palms of your hands.

Heat the oil in a small pot and deep-fry the prepared cubes in a few batches. The oil is ready for frying when it starts bubbling once you drop a piece of tofu, seitan or tempeh in it.

Fry the cubes for 1–2 minutes, until golden brown, then drain on kitchen paper/paper towels on a plate, before using in other recipes. You could also snack on them as they are, add them to a salad, or make skewers with raw or baked veggies.

300 g/10 oz. tofu, seitan or tempeh, cut into 2-cm/ ¾-inch cubes

a handful of plain/all-purpose flour or millet flour, for frying

200 ml/¾ cup sunflower oil, for deep-frying

For the marinade

4 teaspoons tamari

1 teaspoon oil of your choosing (aromatic oils like olive or dark sesame work best)

2 teaspoons Dijon mustard (optional)

2 teaspoons dried herbs or ground spices of your choosing

2 garlic cloves, crushed

Who says you can't enjoy something chocolatey for breakfast, and not feel guilt about it? Cacao powder used in this recipe is raw and unprocessed, containing minerals and antioxidants. In its purest form, we now know that chocolate is good for you! This is great for when you feel like having a milkshake for breakfast. Almond butter is also great to have in the morning since it's a satisfying and healthy fat. If you like, you can add healthy maca powder too, or omit it altogether.

chocolate almond butter
SMOOTHIE

The beauty of this recipe is its simplicity as well as its chocolaty nature. Simply purée all the ingredients in a food processor until smooth.

Serve in a large glass.

Variation If you prefer not to use banana you could substitute frozen pear here. The taste is just as good and pear acts as a natural sweetener which blends beautifully with the chocolate for a super-sweet morning treat.

240 ml/1 cup almond milk (or make your own, see page 15)

1½ tablespoons cacao powder

1 teaspoon maca powder (optional)

2 tablespoons almond butter (or make your own, see page 16)

90 g/¾ cup ice

½ banana

2 teaspoons agave syrup

SERVES 1

Feel like Popeye drinking this vibrant green juice! Spinach contains decent amounts of iron but it's best to eat alongside a food rich in vitamin C to help the body absorb the mineral. Thankfully, oranges provide heaps of vitamin C, as well as a refreshing zesty tang.

POPEYE SPECIAL

6 oranges, peeled and quartered

4 handfuls of spinach

4 handfuls of chopped pointed cabbage

150ml/⅔ cup green tea, cooled

6 basil leaves, chopped

1 teaspoon finely grated orange zest

Juice the oranges, spinach and cabbage, and stir in the cooled green tea and basil leaves. Serve sprinkled with orange zest

SERVES 2

A healthful and delicious combination of dried fruits, oats, nuts, seeds and naturally sweet spices — and, yes, even vegetables! These bars are perfect for sustaining energy levels and giving you a midday boost if you need to survive back-to-back seminars, or stayed out later than expected the night before!

SPICED FRUIT BARS

Put 100 g/¾ cup of the hazelnuts in a food processor and blitz until finely chopped, then add the oats and process again until everything is very finely chopped.

Add the prunes and 50 g/⅓ cup of the apricots and process to a thick, smooth-ish paste, occasionally scraping down the mixture from the sides when needed. Stir in the chia seeds, mixed/apple pie spice, carrot, pumpkin seeds, orange zest and orange juice.

Spoon the fruit mixture into the lined baking pan and spread out with the back of a dampened spoon until it is about 1 cm/½ inch thick.

Cut the remaining apricots into small pieces and scatter over the top. Repeat with the rest of the hazelnuts, pressing the nuts and apricots down slightly to help them stick to the fruit mixture. Chill for 30 minutes to firm up, then cut into 16 bars, each 2 cm/¾ inch wide. Store in the fridge in an airtight container for up to 2 weeks.

115 g/scant 1 cup roasted hazelnuts, roughly chopped

40 g/scant ½ cup jumbo rolled/old fashioned oats

125 g/scant 1 cup pitted dried prunes, chopped

70 g/½ cup soft dried apricots, chopped

1 tablespoon chia seeds

2 teaspoons mixed/apple pie spice

1 carrot, about 50 g/1¾ oz., finely grated

2 tablespoons pumpkin seeds, roughly chopped

finely grated zest and freshly squeezed juice of 1 large orange

a baking pan, lined with clingfilm/plastic wrap

MAKES 16

Not just vegan, these cookies are perfect if you or any of any of your friends need to follow a strict gluten- or soy-free diet. Coconut flour is a low-GI flour and is unique to work with because it soaks up a lot of liquid. You can substitute ripe mashed banana for the fruit purée, it will still be just as tasty!

coconut BREAKFAST COOKIES

½ teaspoon bicarbonate of soda/baking soda

½ teaspoon xanthan gum

1 teaspoon ground cinnamon

170 g/¾ cup chopped pineapple in its juice from a can

65 g/½ cup coconut flour or kamut flour

2 tablespoons flaxseeds/linseeds

2 tablespoons of ground flaxseeds/linseeds mixed with 6 tablespoons of water

1 teaspoon pure vanilla extract

60 ml/¼ cup almond milk (or make your own, see page 15)

60 ml/¼ cup melted coconut butter

30 g/⅓ cup gluten-free rolled/old fashioned oats

2 tablespoons desiccated/dried unsweetened shredded coconut

2 tablespoons pure maple syrup

50 g/⅓ cup chopped dried figs

a baking sheet, lined with baking parchment

Preheat the oven to 180°C (350°F) Gas 4.

Sift the bicarbonate of soda/baking soda, xanthan gum and cinnamon into a mixing bowl.

Roughly purée the pineapple in its juice in a food processor and add to the mix. Add in the remaining ingredients one at a time and stir until the fruit has a good coating of batter. Cover and chill in the fridge for around 20 minutes.

Once chilled, use a tablespoon to measure equally sized balls of cookie dough and space each out on the prepared baking sheet. Press each ball down with your finger to flatten the mix slightly and make an imprint.

Bake for 12–15 minutes until golden and serve.

MAKES APPROXIMATELY 18 COOKIES

SERVES 4

This grain-free recipe is a great cereal option, served hot or cold. You can make the compote in large batches and store it in the freezer ready to thaw and serve in no time. It's also great as a dessert – just heat the fruit, add some vegan yoghurt and you are good to go.

CINNAMON 'GRANOLA'
with pear & cranberry compote

First make the compote. Put the chopped pears, lemon zest and lemon juice into a saucepan. Set over medium heat and simmer for 10–15 minutes, until the fruit becomes soft and breaks up easily when pressed with a spoon. If your pears are a little under ripe, you may need to add a little water (or maple syrup if you have a sweet tooth) to get the right consistency. If you like, you can keep some bits of pears whole.

If you're using fresh cranberries, put 2 tablespoons of maple syrup with 200 ml/¾ cup of water in a separate pan and add the cranberries. Set over medium heat and simmer for 10–15 minutes until the berries break down, and produce a luscious red syrup. Carefully taste the syrup (let cool on a spoon first) and add more maple syrup if desired. Set aside.

Combine the pear and cranberry mixtures (or add dried cranberries to the pear mixture). Transfer to sterilized glass jars, screw on the lids and turn upside down. The pressure of the cooling compote will seal the jars. Alternatively, set aside.

Preheat the oven to 150°C (300°F) Gas 2.

For the granola, mix all the ingredients together in a large bowl so that all the nuts and seeds are coated with syrup and cinnamon. Spread onto the prepared baking sheet and bake in the preheated oven for 10–15 minutes or until golden.

Remove from the oven and set aside to cool. The mixture will crisp up as it cools. Serve with the pear and cranberry compote or store in an airtight container for up to 1 week.

200 g/1¾ cups pecans, roughly chopped

100 g/1¼ cups flaked/slivered almonds

60 g/½ cup mixed chopped nuts

50 g/⅓ cup brown flaxseeds/linseeds

2–3 tablespoons pure maple syrup

2–3 teaspoons ground cinnamon

For the compote

8 pears, cored and roughly chopped

grated zest and freshly squeezed juice of 1 lemon

2–4 tablespoons pure maple syrup

80 g/¾ cup fresh or dried cranberries

sterilized glass jars with airtight lids

a baking sheet, lined with baking parchment

The shiny chia seeds have recently been rediscovered and are referred to as 'an ancient American superfood'. Rich in calcium and omega-3 and -6 fatty acids, they are nutritionally very similar to flax and sesame seeds, and should therefore become part of everybody's diet. This quick porridge will fill your tummy for many hours!

simple & filling
CHIA SEED PORRIDGE

40 g/¼ cup chia seeds

2 tablespoons raisins or other dried fruits

230 ml/1 scant cup nut milk (or make your own, see page 15)

a pinch of sea salt

⅛ teaspoon bourbon vanilla powder or ground cinnamon

2 tablespoons raw or dry-roasted mixed nuts

fresh fruit, chopped (optional)

In a bowl, mix together the chia seeds and dried fruits. Lightly warm the nut milk in a small saucepan, add the salt and vanilla or cinnamon, and pour it over the seeds. Leave it to soak for 10 minutes.

If you only have raw nuts, preheat the oven to 180°C (350°F) Gas 4. Spread the nuts on a baking sheet and roast in the oven for 10–14 minutes, stirring occasionally. When the nuts start cracking and releasing their oils, that's when they're done. Be careful not to burn them, as this can happen easily, so it's best to check them after 8–10 minutes and continue roasting for a couple more minutes if they're not done.

Transfer the nuts onto a plate and wait for them to cool slightly. Chop them coarsely and sprinkle over the porridge, along with a little chopped fresh fruit, if desired.

Note If you have leftover dry-roasted nuts they are great as a healthy snack or as an addition to cakes, cookies, salads – to anything really!

SERVES 1

This oatmeal is the perfect warming bowlful. Combining pumpkin purée and pie spices makes for a welcome morning treat!

pumpkin pie
OATMEAL

Put the milk, spices and pumpkin purée in a small saucepan or pot set over a gentle heat and bring to a simmer.

Add the oats to the pan and bring to the boil. Quickly turn down the heat and simmer for 15–20 minutes, or 5 minutes for quick-cook oats, stirring occasionally. Add the raisins for the last minute of the cooking time and stir so they become plump and warm.

Meanwhile, prepare the pecan and pumpkin seed garnish. Put the pumpkin seeds and pecans in a dry frying pan/skillet set over a low–medium heat. Toast for 5 minutes then remove from the pan and set aside.

When the oatmeal is ready, remove the pan from the heat and add the maple syrup. Mix well and then pour into bowls to serve.

Top with the toasted pumpkin seeds and pecans and enjoy.

Note You can store the toasted seeds and nuts in a sterilized glass jar sealed with an airtight lid for up to 2 weeks.

900 ml/3½ cups almond milk (or make your own, see page 15)

1 teaspoon ground cinnamon

⅛ teaspoon ground nutmeg

⅛ teaspoon ground ginger

⅛ teaspoon ground cloves

160 g/¾ cup pumpkin purée from a can

200 g/2 cups rolled/old-fashioned oats

40 g/¼ cup (dark) raisins

3 tablespoons pure maple syrup

To garnish

2 tablespoons pumpkin seeds

2 tablespoons pecans

a sterilized glass jar with airtight lid

SERVES 4

When a busy week of lectures are over and the weekend finally arrives, celebrate your Saturday mornings with pancakes and lashings of maple syrup – any friends are sure to love these too! By adding wholegrain flours and flaxseeds the nutritional content is upped, but don't be afraid to skimp on the syrup – that's the best bit!

buckwheat & flaxseed
PANCAKES

50 g/⅓ cup potato starch

½ teaspoon bicarbonate of soda/baking soda

1½ teaspoons baking powder

70 g/½ cup buckwheat flour

60 g/½ cup brown rice flour

3 tablespoons milled flaxseeds/linseeds

½ teaspoon sea salt

1 teaspoon ground cinnamon

480 ml/2 cups almond milk (or make your own, see page 15)

2 tablespoons of ground flaxseeds/linseeds mixed with 6 tablespoons of water

1 teaspoon pure vanilla extract

vegetable oil, for shallow frying

pure maple syrup, to taste

a handful of blueberries, to serve (optional)

Sift the potato starch, bicarbonate of soda/baking soda and baking powder into a mixing bowl. Add in the remaining dry ingredients and set aside. In another bowl, combine the almond milk, flaxseed water mixture and vanilla extract. Add the wet into the dry ingredients gradually and beat to a thick batter.

Heat the oil in a frying pan/skillet over a medium–high heat. Drop the batter from a spoon into the pan to form round circles. Cook until small bubbles form on the top of each pancake. Flip and cook for a further 3 minutes or until golden brown in colour.

Serve immediately, stacked on a plate and drizzled with maple syrup. Blueberries make a tasty addition, if desired, and are a powerful antioxidant.

SERVES 2–4

You're sure to love this yummy way of using tofu, and former egg-lovers are especially keen on it since it looks and tastes similar to scrambled eggs. Actually, better than scrambled eggs! You can use different types of veggies, herbs and spices; this is one suggestion for springtime.

TOFU SCRAMBLE

Cut the mushrooms in half lengthways, then cut into thinner wedges. Add the olive oil, onions and salt to the wok or frying pan/skillet and sauté over a medium heat briefly, stirring energetically to prevent sticking.

Add the mushrooms, asparagus, tamari and turmeric and continue stirring with two wooden spoons. When the mushrooms have soaked up a bit of tamari, turn up the heat, add the tofu and stir for another 1–2 minutes. The scramble should be uniformly yellow in colour. At this point you can add the water to make the scramble juicy, and continue cooking for a couple more minutes. However, whether you need water or not depends on how soft your tofu was to begin with – softer types are moist and don't need any water at the end of cooking.

Mix in the dark sesame oil and basil, season with pepper and serve warm, with a nice salad and a few slices of toasted homemade bread.

150 g/2 cups fresh shiitake mushrooms

4 tablespoons olive oil

120 g/1 cup onions sliced into thin half-moons

½ teaspoon sea salt

80 g/1 cup trimmed asparagus, sliced diagonally at the bottom (if using wild asparagus, then only use the soft tops)

2 tablespoons tamari

½ teaspoon ground turmeric

300 g/10 oz. fresh tofu, mashed with a fork

4 tablespoons water, if necessary

1 teaspoon dark sesame oil

½ teaspoon dried basil or 2 tablespoons chopped fresh basil

freshly ground black pepper

SERVES 2–3

If you want to eat healthy breakfasts, they don't have to be all smoothies and baked goods — if you like a savoury, hearty start to your day, or need a dish to satisfy your hunger, this will have you covered.

aubergine
'BACON' SANDWICH

2 avocados, peeled, pitted and roughly chopped

4–8 large slices raw seed bread (such as Lydia's Organic Sunflower Seed Bread) or other bread of your choice

2 large tomatoes, sliced

a handful of alfalfa sprouts

4 tablespoons olive oil

For the aubergine bacon

1 large aubergine/eggplant

1–2 teaspoons sea salt

1 teaspoon liquid smoke (optional)

2 teaspoons smoked paprika

a pinch of chipotle powder

2 tablespoons olive oil

2 tablespoons balsamic vinegar

a dehydrator (optional)

a mandoline grater (optional)

Begin by preparing the aubergine/eggplant bacon. If you want the recipe to be raw, you will need a dehydrator for this recipe. If not, an oven is just fine. Preheat the oven or dehydrator to 110°C (225°F) Gas ¼.

Using a mandoline, slice the aubergine/eggplant into very thin strips and then cut in half lengthways so that the rashers resemble the shape of bacon. If you don't have a mandoline, slice them by hand as thinly as possible, bearing in mind that they needn't be neat. Place the aubergine/eggplant strips in a casserole dish.

Mix the remaining aubergine/eggplant bacon ingredients together in a small mixing bowl with 6 tablespoons of water. Pour the mixture over the aubergine/eggplant rashers. Set aside to soften for about 15 minutes.

Remove the aubergine/eggplant rashers from the dish and place them on a baking sheet or dehydrator sheet, reserving the leftover marinade. Brush the aubergine/eggplant strips lightly with the marinade, then place in the preheated oven or dehydrator. Allow the aubergine/eggplant bacon to get really crispy – in the oven this will take 4–6 hours and in the dehydrator it will take 16–20 hours.

To prepare the sandwiches, lightly mash the avocado onto the bread. Top with slices of tomato, the alfalfa sprouts and 3–4 aubergine/eggplant bacon rashers. You could top with another slice of seed bread or serve as an open sandwich. This sandwich is also delicious with a layer of sauerkraut.

MAKES ABOUT 20–25
AUBERGINE BACON
RASHERS & SERVES 4

SERVES 2–4

These smoky home-made baked beans are the perfect comfort food to enjoy on a winter morning (or cosy night in!). Eat them spooned over toast or in a bowl with some crusty bread on the side for dunking.

home-made
BAKED BEANS

Preheat the oven to 160°C (325°F) Gas 3.

Put the oil, onion and 2 teaspoons of water in a flameproof casserole dish and cover with a lid. Cook gently over a low heat for about 10 minutes, until the onion is soft but has not taken on too much colour.

Add the garlic, brown sugar, treacle, mustard, paprika, vinegar and chilli/chile, if using, and stir until everything is well incorporated. Add the haricot/navy beans, tomatoes and stock. Bring to the boil, cook for 2 minutes then cover with a lid and transfer to the oven. Bake in the middle of the preheated oven for 2 hours. If the consistency is too liquid, put the casserole dish on the stovetop over a gentle heat and reduce the liquid to the desired consistency. Season with salt and pepper. Serve hot with crusty bread or toast.

2 tablespoons olive oil

1 red onion, chopped

2 garlic cloves, crushed

1 tablespoon brown sugar

1 tablespoon black treacle/molasses

1 teaspoon Dijon mustard

½ teaspoon paprika

1 tablespoon balsamic vinegar

½ fresh red chilli/chile, deseeded and finely chopped (optional)

400-g/14-oz. can haricot/navy beans

400-g/14-oz. can chopped tomatoes

240 ml/1 cup vegetable stock

sea salt and freshly ground black pepper

slices of crusty bread or toast with vegan margarine, to serve (optional)

SUPER SNACKS

Kale is one of the best things you can put in your body, and turning them into chips is a brilliant way to sneak them into your diet in a fun way. They are moreish for when that mid-morning hunger hits, but also light enough that you could eat the entire batch in front of a good film without feeling guilty!

spicy tomato
KALE CHIPS

Preheat the oven to 200°C (400°F) Gas 6.

Tear small pieces of kale off the stems and place them in a colander. Wash them, then dry them as thoroughly as possible – ideally they should be completely dry. Place the dry pieces in a large bowl.

Put the tomato quarters and sun-dried tomatoes in a food processor. Pulse until smooth, scraping down the sides of the bowl as you go. It won't seem like a lot of mixture, but the idea is just to flavour the kale rather than cover it in a thick sauce. Add the paprika, cumin and salt, then as much cayenne and black pepper as you like, depending on how spicy you want your chips to turn out. Process the mixture again, then pour it into the bowl of kale. Using your hands, toss the kale so that it is evenly coated in the mixture.

Spread the kale pieces onto the prepared baking sheet and bake in the preheated oven with the door slightly ajar for about 14–16 minutes. You will know the kale is ready when it is totally crispy and thin. If you can resist eating all of the kale immediately, store it in an airtight container for about 4–5 days at room temperature.

1 head of curly kale or 1 bag of pre-chopped curly kale (about 50 g/1¾ oz.)

1 large tomato, quartered

3 sun-dried tomatoes (dry not marinated ones, with no added sugar)

½ teaspoon paprika

¼ teaspoon ground cumin

a pinch of sea salt

⅛–¼ teaspoon cayenne pepper

freshly ground black pepper

a baking sheet, lined with foil

SERVES 2-4

You'll often find that some of the simplest food is also vegan, and this popcorn is no exception — it's easy to make but very, very tasty. The amount of salt and pepper you add is very much down to personal taste, so add gradually and keep tasting until you are happy.

salt & pepper
POPCORN

1–2 tablespoons sunflower or vegetable oil

90 g/⅓ cup mini popcorn kernels

sea salt and freshly ground black pepper

MAKES 1 LARGE BOWL

Heat the oil in a large lidded saucepan with a few popcorn kernels in the pan. When you hear the kernels pop, carefully tip in the rest of the kernels. Shake the pan over the heat until the popping stops. Take care when lifting the lid as any unpopped kernels may still pop from the heat of the pan.

Tip the popcorn into a bowl, removing any unpopped kernels as you go.

Season the popcorn well with salt and pepper (about a teaspoon of each is about right) and serve warm or cold.

For some, onion rings evoke nostalgic memories of childhood meals. Before we even taste something, the anticipation of it influences our eventual enjoyment of the food, which is perhaps why this grown-up healthier version of the fried snack is a real crowd-pleaser.

jalapeño ONION RINGS

Preheat the oven to 220°C (425°F) Gas 7.

Mix the flaxseeds/linseeds with 175 ml/²/₃ cup water and set aside. Separately, mix the cornmeal, cracker crumbs, jalapeño, salt and pepper to taste in a wide bowl.

Separate the onion slices into rings. Dip them into the flaxseed/linseed mixture, then into the crumb mixture. For each onion ring, do this twice so that they are double-coated.

Arrange the rings on the prepared baking sheets and bake in the preheated oven for 8–12 minutes until they are slightly browned on the outside and cooked all the way through. If liked, serve with tomato ketchup.

3 tablespoons ground flaxseeds/linseeds

170 g/1 cup cornmeal

150 g/1 cup cracker crumbs

1 large fresh jalapeño pepper, thinly sliced and deseeded if you don't like things too spicy

½ teaspoon sea salt

2 large onions, cut into 2-cm/1-inch thick slices

freshly ground black pepper

2 baking sheets, lined with foil

MAKES ABOUT 36 RINGS

Food brings people together, especially for larger shared events, like Christmas and Halloween. This vegan take on chicken wings is perfect for watching a sports event with friends; a junk-y treat made with veggies.

almond-crusted
BUFFALO BITES

85 g/¾ cup coconut flour

30 g/¼ cup ground almonds (or use more coconut flour)

1 teaspoon garlic powder

1½ teaspoons onion powder

½ teaspoon sea salt

1 large head of cauliflower, cut into florets

1 tablespoon olive oil

150 ml/⅔ cup hot sauce (such as Frank's RedHot)

For the cashew mayo

120 g/1 cup cashew nuts, soaked for 2 hours and drained

2 tablespoons freshly squeezed lemon juice

2 tablespoons apple cider vinegar

¾ teaspoon sea salt

1 teaspoon agave or pure maple syrup

a baking sheet, greased and lined with baking parchment

Preheat the oven to 220°C (425°F) Gas 7.

In a large mixing bowl, combine the coconut flour, ground almonds, if using, garlic and onion powders and salt with 250 ml/1 cup of water.

Dip each cauliflower floret individually into the mixture so that it's fully coated. Place them on the prepared baking sheet and bake in the preheated oven for 15 minutes.

Meanwhile, beat the olive oil and hot sauce together in a bowl. Remove the cauliflower from the oven and dip each floret in the hot sauce mixture, making sure they are well coated. Return to the oven for another 20 minutes.

To make the cashew mayo, place the cashews, lemon juice, cider vinegar, sea salt and agave or maple syrup in a food processor or blender and blend until smooth. With the motor running, drizzle in 4–6 tablespoons of water, one at a time, until you have a thick dipping consistency.

Serve the baked cauliflower with the cashew mayo as an appetizer, snack or as a side dish for a main course.

SERVES 8

This recipe will be the hummus you keep coming back to time and time again — shop-bought tubs will be a thing of the past, guaranteed! Cooking dried chickpeas is highly recommended for an extra-fresh hummus, but using canned chickpeas and their liquid is a quick and easy alternative!

BASIC HUMMUS

Put all the ingredients in a food processor or blender, except the extra chickpeas and olive oil to serve, and blend, slowly adding the cooking liquid until you reach a thick and creamy consistency; this will take about 1 minute. High-speed blenders make the creamiest texture and need less liquid and time, but both food processors and stick blenders can be used as well. Adjust the lemon juice and salt to taste.

Serve topped with 2 tablespoons extra-virgin olive oil and 2 tablespoons whole chickpeas. Garnish with chopped flat-leaf parsley, if you like.

320 g/2¼ cups cooked chickpeas, plus 60 ml/¼ cup of the cooking liquid, or more if needed, plus 2 tablespoons cooked chickpeas to serve

2 tablespoons extra-virgin olive oil, plus 2 tablespoons to serve

1 tablespoon tahini

3 garlic cloves

freshly squeezed juice of ½ lemon, or to taste

½ teaspoon sea salt, or to taste

chopped fresh flat-leaf parsley, to garnish (optional)

MAKES ABOUT 2–4 SERVINGS

Chickpea/gram flour is used all over Europe to make soft-yet-crunchy fritters. In Sicily, they're called panelle. In Liguria, they're panissa or panizza, while in Nice, they're known as panisses and are much like chunky fries.

CHICKPEA FRITTERS

250 g/2 cups chickpea/gram flour, sifted

1 teaspoon sea salt

1 tablespoon chopped fresh flat-leaf parsley

3 tablespoons olive oil

coarse sea salt and freshly ground black pepper

SERVES 4–6

Beat the chickpea/gram flour into 1 litre/4¼ cups of water until there are no lumps, then season with the salt.

Heat the batter gently in a saucepan, stirring constantly, until it boils and thickens. Simmer the mixture for about 15 minutes, beating constantly, as lumps tend to form otherwise. Stir in the parsley and cook for another 5 minutes.

Pour into an oiled 30 x 20-cm/12 x 8-inch baking sheet, and smooth out the surface. The mixture should be no more than 1 cm/½ inch thick. Let cool for several hours to allow the mixture to solidify.

Preheat the oven to 200°C (400°F) Gas 6. When the batter has cooled and solidified, cut into triangles, squares or, to make chunky chips, batons about the size of your largest finger.

When the oven is hot, put the olive oil in a clean baking sheet and heat in the oven for a few minutes, then using a spatula, transfer the triangles, squares or batons to the hot oil, carefully flipping over once to coat both sides with oil. Put in the oven for about 20 minutes, until the fritters are crisp on the surface and starting to brown, then turn over and cook for another 10 minutes.

Alternatively, heat some oil in a frying pan/skillet, and fry the fritters on the hob/stovetop.

Sprinkle with coarse sea salt and black pepper and serve immediately, either as a snack with drinks or with a salad.

These small, delicate bites are a real treat not only because of their fresh taste but also because the bright red and light green combination of colours really gets noticed! You can eat them as appetizers, or pop them in an airtight container to snack on during the day.

CHERRY TOMATOES
filled with spinach pesto

Wash the tomatoes and remove their stems. If you like, cut a very thin layer off the bottom of each tomato so that they can sit on a serving plate without rolling. Slice off the tops and scoop out the flesh with a small spoon to make enough space for the filling. Be careful not to damage the tomatoes.

Wash and drain the spinach well. Lightly dry-roast the sunflower seeds in a small pan to release their full aroma. Place all the ingredients (except the tomatoes) in a food processor or blender and blend until smooth. Add 1–2 tablespoons water if necessary; the pesto should be liquid enough to be easily spooned or piped into the cored cherry tomatoes.

Fill each tomato carefully and serve immediately or pop in an airtight container to eat as a snack on the go.

Tip If you can get your hands on it, use wild garlic (bear's garlic) instead of spinach for a beautiful aroma and an even more fluorescent green colour! Other soft greens and herbs work well, too. Also, you can use almonds, pine nuts, hazelnuts, sesame seeds, cashews and any other nuts and seeds instead of sunflower seeds to make this pesto.

20 cherry tomatoes

2 handfuls of baby spinach

85 g/⅔ cup sunflower seeds

4 tablespoons olive oil

2 garlic cloves, peeled

1 teaspoon freshly squeezed lemon juice (to prevent oxidation of greens)

sea salt

MAKES 20

This is a deliciously simple pâté that looks wonderfully dramatic. You will find that it has a pleasing kick from the chilli/chile and fresh ginger.

BEET PÂTÉ

1 beet(root)

1 small red (bell) pepper, deseeded

½ fresh red chilli/chile

1 tablespoon peeled and chopped fresh ginger

200 g/1⅔ cups cashew nuts

2 tablespoons olive oil

2 tablespoons nama shoyu (unpasteurized soy sauce)

2 tablespoons apple cider vinegar

1 tablespoon pure maple syrup

sea salt

Peel the beet(root) and chop into 2-cm/¾-inch chunks, and roughly chop the (bell) pepper and chilli/chile.

Put all the ingredients in a food processor and blitz until very smooth.

Serve chilled, with crackers.

SERVES 4

There is something irresistible about these dainty, crisp-textured potato straws. Serve them as a night-in snack or as a replacement for store-bought crisps/chips.

piquant
POTATO STRAWS

Peel the potatoes and cut into short, thin matchstick strips. Rinse in cold water, then pat dry thoroughly.

Heat enough oil for deep-frying in a deep pan or wok to 180°C/350°F or until a small piece of bread added to the hot oil browns within 60 seconds.

Fry the potato straws in batches, so as not to overcrowd the pan. Cook them until they turn golden brown on all sides, remove with a slotted spoon and drain on kitchen paper/paper towels on a plate.

Toss the freshly fried potato straws at once with the two types of paprika or pimentón and salt, to taste, mixing thoroughly. Serve at once.

400 g/14 oz. potatoes

1 teaspoon hot smoked paprika or pimentón

1 teaspoon mild smoked paprika or pimentón

1–2 teaspoons sea salt

oil, for deep-frying

If you're looking for an instant falafel recipe that requires minimal prep, check out these crunchy beauties! Serving them with a fair amount of sauce is key, since the use of chickpea/gram flour, instead of soaked chickpeas, results in an ever so slightly drier consistency.

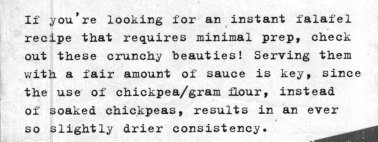

chickpea flour & harissa
PATTIES

120 g/1 cup chickpea/gram flour

¼ teaspoon bicarbonate of soda/ baking soda

½ teaspoon sea salt

½ teaspoon ground coriander

1 teaspoon harissa powder (or to taste)

¼ teaspoon dried oregano

30 g/1 tablespoon very finely chopped onion

80 ml/⅓ cup hot water

3 tablespoons coconut oil (or other oil), for frying

harissa paste and Tofu Mayonnaise (see page 20), to serve (optional)

SERVES ABOUT 4–8

Combine the flour with the other dry ingredients, mix in the chopped onion and slowly start incorporating the hot water. You should get a non-sticky dough that can be shaped easily. Let the mixture sit for 10 minutes before forming it into small patties.

Heat the oil in a non-stick frying pan/ skillet over a medium heat. Depending on the size of your pan you will need to fry them in at least two batches. Make sure not to overcrowd the pan. Lower the heat and let the falafels fry for 3–4 minutes on each side, or until golden brown. If you wish to build your spicy food tolerance, serve these with plenty of harissa paste, as well as tofu mayonnaise to cool!

LOVE YOUR LUNCHES

MAKES 12 FALAFELS

Chickpeas aren't the only legumes you can soak to create tasty falafel. Red lentils are also an option – they make a falafel that is softer and easier to digest, and the soaking time is shorter! Feel free to use any spices and any type of soft greens you can lay your hands on!

red lentil
FALAFEL WRAPS

Wash the red lentils thoroughly and let soak in plenty of water overnight. Drain, rinse well and let drain again for 5 minutes. It's best to use a food processor fitted with an 'S' blade for blending the falafel mix, even though it can also be done in a good blender. Blend all the ingredients (except the frying oil) until you get a paste – the texture should resemble coarse sand.

Roll into walnut-sized balls, then pat them down just a little to get chubby oval-shaped falafels. To prevent sticking, wet your hands while shaping.

Heat the oil in a small pan and deep-fry the falafels for 4 minutes or until nicely browned. Because we're using soaked lentils, these falafels need to be deep-fried to make them digestible – baking them wouldn't work.

To assemble, warm the tortillas in the oven, add some lettuce and 4 or 5 falafels on top of each one, together with two tablespoons each of the salsa and guacamole. Wrap up and serve with extra dips. Or, even better, put all the ingredients on the table and let everyone make their own wraps!

90 g/½ cup split red lentils

40 g/1 cup finely chopped chard or spinach

2 garlic cloves

½ teaspoon sea salt

1 teaspoon finely chopped fresh ginger

1 teaspoon curry powder

½ teaspoon ground coriander

½ teaspoon ground turmeric

½ teaspoon garam masala

½ teaspoon ground ginger

⅛ teaspoon chilli/chili powder (or to taste)

230 ml/1 cup oil, for deep-frying

To serve

wholegrain tortillas

young lettuce leaves

Tomato Salsa (see page 84)

Lighter Guacamole (see page 19)

A good-quality vegan sandwich can be eaten for breakfast, lunch or dinner, and if the ingredients are well chosen, you'll be getting all the necessary nutrients. The three main components of a satisfying sandwich are: tasty bread, seasoned protein and freshly pickled vegetables — the combinations are endless!

fried
TOFU SANDWICHES

240 g/8¼ oz. tofu, seitan or tempeh, marinated and fried (see page 27)

To serve

fresh crusty bread rolls or a large seeded baguette

4 tablespoons spread of your choosing (Tofu Mayonnaise, see page 20, Lighter Guacamole, see page 19, Cashew Mayo, see page 56)

2 handfuls of lettuce or other salad greens

4 tablespoons seed sprouts

sliced pickles or kimchi (optional)

roasted red peppers (optional)

To prepare the tofu, seitan or tempeh, cut four 10 x 6-cm/ 4 x 2½-inch slices, 6 mm/¼ inch thick. Marinate and fry these slices following the instructions on page 27. You don't have to deep-fry the slices; just cover the bottom of the pan with oil and fry them on both sides until browned.

When you're ready to assemble the sandwich, cut two rolls in half crossways in the middle or a large baguette crossways in the middle, then lengthways to get 2 sandwiches. First add the spread on the bottom slices, then add 2 slices of fried tofu, seitan or tempeh, sprinkle with salad and seed sprouts and top with the remaining slices of bread. Add sliced pickles or kimchi and roasted red peppers to the sandwich, if liked, or serve on the side.

Eat immediately or wrap in clingfilm/plastic wrap and eat when you're hungry!

SERVES 2

Po' boys are a traditional type of sandwich from Louisiana in the US, and this vegan take on the usually meat-based recipe shows that vegan food can be a delicious and creative cuisine.

roasted aubergine
PO' BOYS

Preheat the oven to 200°C (400°F) Gas 6.

Brush the aubergine/eggplant slices on both sides with oil and spread out on the prepared baking sheet. Sprinkle with a little of the Cajun spice mix to give a light coating.

Roast in the preheated oven for about 15 minutes. Flip the aubergine/eggplant slices over and sprinkle the other side with Cajun spice mix. Bake for another 10 minutes, until soft and golden.

To make the white bean purée, combine all the ingredients in a food processor or blender with salt to taste, and blend until smooth. Add the cold water for a smoother consistency.

Combine the slaw ingredients in a bowl and season to taste with salt.

Assemble the sandwiches with a good slathering of white bean purée on the baguettes, topped with the roasted aubergine/eggplant slices and herby slaw.

MAKES 2–3 BIG SANDWICHES OR 4 SMALLER ONES

For the aubergine/eggplant

1 large aubergine/eggplant, sliced into 1.5-cm/½-inch thick rounds

avocado or olive oil, for brushing

1–2 tablespoons Cajun spice mix

For the white bean purée

160 g/1¼ cups canned white beans, drained and rinsed

1 tablespoon tahini

1 tablespoon freshly squeezed lemon juice

½ garlic clove, peeled

¼ teaspoon chilli flakes/ hot red pepper flakes

¼ teaspoon smoked paprika

1–2 tablespoons ice-cold water (optional)

sea salt

For the herby slaw

60 g/1 cup thinly sliced red cabbage

20 g/½ tightly packed cup flat-leaf parsley or coriander/ cilantro leaves (or a mixture), finely chopped

½ garlic clove, finely grated

1 tablespoon olive oil

2 teaspoons apple cider vinegar

To serve

fresh baguettes, cut into 15-cm/ 6-inch lengths and split in half

a baking sheet, lined with baking parchment

This makes a light change from some heavier taco fillings - ideal for a lunch that doesn't make you feel sleepy for the rest of the day!

ancho-roasted
SQUASH TACOS

1 large onion, halved and sliced

4 tablespoons vegetable oil

2 teaspoons ground cumin

2 teaspoons dried oregano

2 teaspoons ancho chilli/chili powder

1 teaspoon fine sea salt

a good pinch of ground cinnamon

1.2 kg/2 lb. 12 oz. butternut squash, peeled and cubed

8–12 corn or flour tortillas, warmed

To serve

vegan sour cream or yoghurt

sprigs of fresh coriander/cilantro

Lighter Guacamole (see page 19)

hot sauce (such as Tabasco)

lemon wedges

Preheat the oven to 220°C (425°F) Gas 7.

To prepare the squash, combine the onion slices, oil, cumin, oregano, chilli/chile powder, salt and cinnamon in a large bowl. Add the squash and toss well to coat evenly.

Spread the spiced squash mixture on a baking sheet large enough to hold it in a single layer. Roast in the preheated oven for 25–35 minutes until well browned.

To serve, put a generous helping of squash in the middle of each tortilla. Top with a spoonful of vegan sour cream and scatter over a few sprigs of fresh coriander/cilantro. Serve immediately with the guacamole, hot sauce and lemon wedges on the side for squeezing.

SERVES 4–6

Avocados continue to reign supreme in the world of breakfast, lunch and brunch in-between! If you can get hold of it, a nutty dukkah adds great texture and saltiness to counter-balance the creaminess of the avocado, and the courgette/zucchini salad gives it a wonderful freshness.

SMASHED AVO ON TOAST
with raw courgettes & dukkah

Cut the avocados in half, remove the stones/pits and scoop out the flesh into a bowl. Roughly mash the flesh with a fork, keeping it quite chunky. Add the lemon juice with a generous pinch of sea salt and black pepper. Gently combine.

To make the courgette/zucchini salad, use a mandoline or vegetable peeler to slice the courgette/zucchini into long thin ribbons. Place into a bowl with the herb leaves, olive oil, lemon zest and a pinch of salt and pepper. Toss together.

Spread the smashed avocado generously onto the two slices of toast. Heap the courgette/zucchini salad on top and sprinkle with the dukkah.

2 ripe avocados

1 tablespoon freshly squeezed lemon juice

1 small courgette/zucchini (approx. 100 g/3½ oz.)

15 g/½ oz. mixed fresh herb leaves, such as mint, coriander/cilantro and flat-leaf parsley

2 teaspoons extra-virgin olive oil

1 teaspoon grated lemon zest

2 slices of sourdough bread, toasted

2 tablespoons dukkah mix

sea salt and freshly ground black pepper

a mandolin grater (optional)

SERVES 2

Some days we need an extra boost, and this bowl full of ultra-healthy goodies is just the answer. For the best results keep the dressing separate and pour over just before serving.

'pick-me-up' POWER BOWL

75 g/½ cup spelt berries

50 g/⅓ cup cooked chickpeas

2 tablespoons pumpkin seeds

½ crisp apple

½ avocado

2 tablespoons freshly squeezed lemon juice

2-cm/¾-inch piece fresh ginger, peeled

2 tablespoons avocado oil

1 tablespoon sunflower oil

1 teaspoon agave syrup

a handful of baby kale leaves

a handful of sprouted seeds

2 tablespoons dried cranberries

sea salt and freshly ground black pepper

Place the spelt berries in a saucepan of cold water, bring to the boil and simmer gently for about 40 minutes until the berries are al dente. Drain, refresh under cold water and shake dry.

Drain the chickpeas, wash in a sieve/strainer and shake dry. Toast the pumpkin seeds in a dry frying pan/skillet for 2 minutes until they start to brown.

Cut the apple into thin batons. Peel, stone/pit and thinly slice the avocado. Add a little lemon juice to the apples and avocado and toss gently. This will help them to keep their colour.

Finely grate the ginger and combine with the avocado oil, sunflower oil, remaining lemon juice and agave syrup. Season to taste with salt and pepper.

Arrange all the ingredients neatly in a round plastic bowl or container, placing the sliced avocado on top with the cranberries. Chill in the refrigerator until required. Just before serving, drizzle over the dressing.

Tip If it's possible, slice the apple and avocado just before serving to keep them extra fresh.

SERVES 1

Freekeh's slightly chewy texture and nutty flavour contrasts nicely with the tomato and avocado in this simple, Middle Eastern-inspired salad. You can eat this as a side to a bigger meal or on its own for lunch.

TOMATO, FREEKEH & AVOCADO SALAD

Cook the freekeh in a pan of boiling, salted water, simmering for 15–20 minutes until tender. Drain and let cool.

Using a sharp knife, cut the avocado in half, turning it as you do to cut around the stone/pit. Twist the two halves to separate. Remove the stone/pit, scoop out the flesh and dice the flesh. In a small bowl, toss with a little of the lemon juice to prevent any discolouration.

Mix together the cooked freekeh, cherry tomatoes, sun-dried tomatoes and spring onion/scallion. Toss with the oil, the remaining lemon juice and parsley. Fold in the diced avocado, top with pine nuts and serve at once.

100 g/⅔ cup freekeh
(a cracked, roasted green wheat)

1 ripe avocado

freshly squeezed juice of ½ lemon

12 cherry tomatoes, quartered

2 sun-dried tomatoes in oil, chopped

1 spring onion/scallion, finely chopped

2 tablespoons argan oil
(or other nut oil such as walnut or groundnut/peanut oil)

2 tablespoons chopped fresh flat-leaf parsley

1 tablespoon pine nuts, toasted

SERVES 4

This spicy bean chilli/chili is served with charred sweetcorn and a fresh and zingy salsa. If you don't have time to char the sweetcorn you can just use a spoonful or two of canned sweetcorn in its place. This makes a large pan-full but it freezes well so if you do not need to feed four, freeze any leftovers in individual portions.

three bean chilli
BAKED POTATO

4 large baking potatoes

1 corn on the cob/ear of corn, peeled

a little olive oil

For the chilli

1 tablespoon olive oil

1 small onion, finely chopped

1 red chilli/chile, deseeded and finely chopped

2 garlic cloves, sliced

400-g/14-oz. can cannellini beans

300-g/10½-oz. can haricot/navy beans

400-g/14-oz. can chopped tomatoes

70 g/2½ oz. tomato purée/paste

400-g/14-oz. can kidney beans in chilli/chili sauce

1 teaspoon paprika

sea salt and freshly ground black pepper

For the tomato salsa

3 tomatoes, deseeded and chopped

1 ripe avocado, peeled, stoned/pitted and chopped

2 spring onions/scallions, thinly sliced

freshly squeezed juice of 1 lime

1 tablespoon olive oil

Preheat the oven to 200°C (400°F) Gas 6.

Prick the skin of your potatoes and rub with a little salt. Place in the oven for about 1 hour, or until the middle of the potato is soft when inserted with a sharp knife.

Meanwhile, brush the corn on the cob with a little oil, place in a hot griddle pan and cook for about 15 minutes until the corn has started to char on all sides. Remove from the heat and let cool.

For the chilli, heat the olive oil in a pan and sauté the onion, chilli/chile and garlic until the onion has softened. Rinse the cannellini and haricot/navy beans under cold water and add them to the pan. Then add the tomatoes, 250 ml/1 cup of water, the kidney beans and sauce, the tomato purée/paste and paprika and season with salt and pepper. Simmer for 30 minutes over a gentle heat until the sauce thickens.

For the salsa, add all of the ingredients to a small bowl and toss everything together. Season, then cover and chill in the fridge until served.

Place the corn on a chopping board and with a sharp knife, cut the kernels off, in slices.

To serve, cut the potatoes open and top each with a portion of chilli. Top with the salsa and corn slices and serve.

ONE-BOWL WONDERS

A fruity, feisty and flavoursome bean stew, this dish is a firm favourite among vegans and devout meat-eaters alike! If you use a Baharat spice blend that contains allspice berries, this dish will have a distinctly Moroccan feel.

fruity
AFRICAN BEAN STEW

Thoroughly rinse the lentils and quinoa and put in a saucepan of boiling unsalted water.

Reduce the heat to a gentle simmer and add the Baharat spice blend. Cook, uncovered, for 20 minutes, or until thick. Drain well.

Heat the oil in the stovetop casserole dish and gently fry the onions and garlic until softened but not brown.

Add the chopped tomatoes and the cooked lentils and quinoa. Stir well, add the vegetable stock and then bring back to a gentle simmer.

Add the African-style hot sauce, bay leaves, thyme, apricots, sultanas/golden raisins, chillies/chiles, mixed beans, (bell) peppers and chickpeas. Stir well. Bring to the boil, then reduce the heat to a very gentle simmer and cook, covered, for at least 1 hour. Stir occasionally.

Add more stock if it looks too dry, but allow the sauce to thicken. Season with salt and pepper at the end of cooking.

Serve with couscous, brown rice or fresh bread.

200 g/generous 1 cup red split lentils

100 g/⅔ cup quinoa

1 teaspoon Baharat (or similar North African) spice blend

1 tablespoon olive oil

2 onions, chopped

6 garlic cloves, crushed

2 x 400-g/14-oz. cans chopped tomatoes

600 ml/2½ cups vegetable stock

3 tablespoons African-style hot chilli/chili or pepper sauce

2 fresh bay leaves

a generous sprig of fresh thyme

75 g/½ cup chopped dried apricots

75 g/½ cup sultanas/golden raisins

hot red chillies/chiles, chopped – as many as you like!

2 x 400-g/14-oz. cans mixed beans, drained

2 ripe red (bell) peppers, deseeded and cut into strips

400-g/14-oz. can chickpeas, drained

sea salt and freshly ground black pepper

couscous, brown rice or fresh bread, to serve

a stovetop casserole dish with lid

SERVES 8

Although carrots may not make you see in the dark, they can offer you a comforting pick-me-up in the form of this carrot and ginger soup, accompanied by a crusty baguette filled with creamy hummus and a crunchy carrot pickle.

CARROT & GINGER SOUP
with hummus & pickled carrot baguettes

1 tablespoon olive oil

1 small onion, finely chopped

1 tablespoon grated fresh ginger

500 g/1 lb. 2 oz. carrots, chopped

1 litre/quart vegetable stock

25 g/1 oz. fresh coriander/cilantro leaves

freshly squeezed juice of 1 large orange

sea salt and freshly ground black pepper

For the carrot pickle

1 carrot, peeled and trimmed

2 tablespoons white wine vinegar

2 teaspoons caster/granulated sugar

1 teaspoon cumin seeds

a pinch of sea salt

For the sandwiches

1 medium baguette

150 g/5½ oz. hummus (or make your own, see page 59)

a handful of spinach leaves

a handful of fresh coriander/cilantro leaves

For the pickle, use a swivel or vegetable peeler to make long strips of carrot. Place in a bowl with the vinegar and sugar. In a dry frying pan/skillet heat the cumin seeds until they start to pop, taking care that you do not burn them. Add to the bowl with the salt and stir so that the sugar and salt dissolve and the carrot strips are all coated in the pickling juices. Leave for about 1 hour to soak.

For the soup, heat the olive oil in a large saucepan/pot and fry the chopped onion until soft and translucent. Add the grated ginger and fry for a further 1–2 minutes. Add the chopped carrots to the pan with the stock, coriander/cilantro leaves and orange juice, and simmer until the carrots are soft. Place in a blender or food processor and blitz to a smooth purée. Return to the pan to keep warm and season with salt and pepper to taste.

When you are ready to serve, pour the soup into warm bowls. Cut the baguette into four portions and slice each one in half horizontally. Fill with the hummus, spinach and coriander/cilantro leaves. Drain the pickling liquid from the carrots and add some of the carrot ribbons to each sandwich. Serve straight away.

SERVES 4

Here is a tasty sauce to whizz up and serve with noodles for a speedy bite at any time of day. This can be served immediately, but it is especially nice served cold, as a noodle salad, so make ahead and chill if there is time. For a more complete meal, serve with stir-fried cubes of tofu on top (see page 27) alongside a green vegetable, such as broccoli, or grab a bottle of sweet chilli/chili sauce.

NOODLES
with sesame-peanut sauce

250 g/9 oz. soba noodles

2–3 spring onions/scallions, sliced on the angle

2–3 tablespoons toasted sesame seeds

For the sauce

4 tablespoons smooth peanut butter (or make your own, see page 16)

30 g/¼ cup unsalted peanuts

leaves from a few sprigs of fresh basil

leaves from a sprig of fresh mint

leaves from a few sprigs of fresh coriander/cilantro

freshly squeezed juice of 1 lime

65 ml/¼ cup rapeseed oil

1 tablespoon sesame oil

1–2 tablespoons sweet chilli/chili sauce, to taste

2 tablespoons silken tofu

1–2 teaspoons soy sauce, to taste

To make the sauce, put the peanut butter, peanuts, basil, mint, coriander/cilantro, lime juice, both oils, chilli/chili sauce, tofu and soy sauce in a food processor or blender and blend to obtain a coarse paste. Taste and add more chilli/chili sauce and/or soy sauce as required.

Cook the noodles according to the package instructions and drain well. Toss the sauce with the warm noodles and add the spring onions/scallions and sesame seeds. Serve warm or cold, as preferred.

Variation This sauce also makes a good dip for vegetables, either raw or lightly steamed. To serve, put the sauce in a small bowl and stir in the toasted sesame seeds. Offer a bowl of sweet chilli/chili sauce alongside and a platter of prepared vegetables, such as broccoli, mangetout/snow peas, carrots, sweet potato and red (bell) peppers.

MAKES 2–4 SERVINGS

This hearty and flavoursome dish is traditionally eaten on the first day of Chinese New Year – Buddhists believe that meat should not be eaten on the first five days of the year.

BUDDHA'S DELIGHT

½ teaspoon Chinese five-spice powder

250 g/8 oz. firm tofu, cut into 2-cm/¾-inch cubes

2 tablespoons vegetable oil

3 garlic cloves, crushed

200 g/7 oz. small broccoli florets

200 g/7 oz. miniature or baby pak choi/bok choy, halved

200 g/7 oz. mangetout/snow peas

1 large carrot, cut into matchsticks

1 red (bell) pepper, deseeded and cut into matchsticks

85 g/3 oz. canned water chestnuts, drained and sliced

85 g/3 oz. canned sliced bamboo shoots, drained and rinsed

rice or noodles, to serve

For the sauce

2 tablespoons tamari or vegan 'fish' sauce

2 tablespoons light soy sauce

125 ml/½ cup vegetable stock

1 tablespoon cornflour/cornstarch, combined with 2 tablespoons cold water

Combine all the sauce ingredients in a bowl and set aside.

Sprinkle the five-spice powder over the tofu.

Heat the oil in a wok or large frying pan/skillet until hot. Add the tofu in batches and stir-fry over a high heat until golden all over. Remove the tofu from the wok and drain well on kitchen paper/paper towels on a plate.

Add the garlic to the wok and stir-fry for 1 minute, or until golden. Add the broccoli, pak choi/bok choi, mangetout/snow peas, carrot and red pepper with a sprinkle of water and stir-fry over a high heat for 2–3 minutes. Finally, throw in the water chestnuts and bamboo shoots.

Pour the sauce into the wok and bring to the boil, then reduce the heat and simmer gently for 2 minutes, or until the sauce has thickened. Divide between 4 bowls and serve with cooked rice or noodles.

SERVES 4

Tahini is a smooth sesame seed paste and a wholesome source of good fats; something required in any balanced diet. Here, it is the magic ingredient that makes this sauce creamy – you'll never notice the absence of oil!

ginger, peas & tahini
PASTA

Cook the peas in a pan of boiling water until soft but still bright green. Drain and set aside.

Dry-fry the ginger and garlic with a pinch of salt in a frying pan/skillet until fragrant, then add the soy sauce, tahini, chopped date and cream, and bring to the boil, beating vigorously. Add a little hot water if necessary – the sauce needs to be thick but not sticky.

Pour the sauce over the cooked pasta, season with black pepper, mix well to incorporate, taste and add more soy sauce and/or salt if needed. Stir in the peas and spring onions/scallions, leaving some peas and onion greens sauce-free so that the bright green colour stays intact. Serve immediately and garnish with some garden cress, if liked.

130 g/1 cup fresh or frozen peas

1 tablespoon very finely chopped fresh ginger

2 garlic cloves, finely chopped

2 tablespoons soy sauce, or to taste

4 tablespoons tahini

1 soft pitted date, very finely chopped

240 ml/1 cup oat or soy cream

160 g/2 cups penne pasta, cooked until al dente

4 spring onions/scallions, finely chopped

sea salt and freshly ground black pepper

garden cress, to garnish

SERVES 2

95

This warm salad is packed with robust flavours as well as nourishing ingredients. The kale is roasted in the oven and needs stirring into the salad just before serving so it stays nice and crisp.

MARINATED MUSHROOM,
crispy kale & rice salad

100 g/½ cup brown basmati rice, rinsed

1 teaspoon ground turmeric

3 tablespoons dark soy sauce

2 tablespoons sweet chilli/chili sauce

300 g/11 oz. chestnut/cremini mushrooms, sliced

175 g/6 oz. curly kale, tough stalks removed and leaves torn into large bite-sized pieces

2 teaspoons sesame oil

2 tablespoons coconut oil

2 handfuls of unsalted roasted cashews, roughly chopped

sea salt and freshly ground black pepper

Cook the rice following the package instructions, stirring the turmeric into the cooking water. Drain, if necessary, and leave to stand, covered, for 10 minutes.

Meanwhile, mix together the soy sauce and sweet chilli/chili sauce in a bowl. Add the mushrooms and toss until coated in the marinade, then set aside.

Preheat the oven to 150°C (300°F) Gas 2. Toss the kale in the sesame oil and spread out on 1–2 baking sheets. Roast for 15 minutes, turning once, until crisp but not browned; keep an eye on it as it can easily burn.

Heat the coconut oil in a large frying pan/skillet over a medium-high heat and fry the mushrooms for 5 minutes. Pour off and retain any liquid from the mushrooms as this will form the dressing for the salad. Return the pan to the heat and cook the mushrooms for another 5 minutes, until they start to crisp.

Transfer the rice to a serving bowl and add the mushrooms and the cooking juices. Stir until combined and season, if necessary. Just before serving, stir in the crispy kale and sprinkle the cashews over the top.

SERVES 4

This recipe is based on a Moroccan-style stew. It is a very versatile dish so you can use whatever veggies you have to hand. For a satisfying meal, serve with plenty of couscous.

VEGETABLE TAGINE

Preheat the oven to 180°C (350°F) Gas 4.

Heat the oil in a flameproof casserole dish set over a low–medium heat. Add the onion and cook for 5 minutes. Add the turmeric, cinnamon, paprika, ginger, chilli/chile, garlic and orange zest, and cook for 1 minute. Then add the (bell) peppers, sweet potato, aubergine/eggplant and carrots. Stir so that they are well covered with the spice mixture and cook for 2 minutes.

Stir in the apricots, tomatoes, syrup and chickpeas. Then add the vegetable stock. Bring to the boil and cook on the stovetop for 2 minutes. Cover with a lid and transfer to the preheated oven to bake for 30–40 minutes. When the tagine is cooked, remove from the oven and stir in the spinach.

Spoon the tagine onto serving plates with cooked couscous and top with chopped fresh coriander/cilantro mixed in yoghurt, if you like. Serve hot.

SERVES 4–6

2 tablespoons olive oil

2 red onions, quartered

1 teaspoon each ground turmeric and cinnamon

½ teaspoon paprika

1-cm/½-inch piece of fresh ginger, peeled and finely chopped

1 red chilli/chile, finely chopped

2 garlic cloves, crushed

grated zest of 1 orange

1 red and 1 yellow (bell) pepper, roughly chopped

1 sweet potato, cubed

1 aubergine/eggplant, cut into chunks

2 carrots, sliced

50 g/⅓ cup dried apricots, quartered

400-g/14-oz. can chopped tomatoes

1 tablespoon pure maple syrup

400-g/14-oz. can chickpeas, drained

500 ml/2 cups vegetable stock

a large handful of baby spinach

To serve

a handful of chopped fresh coriander/cilantro stirred into vegan yoghurt (optional)

couscous

This is a great mid-week curry and perfect for when you're in need of rejuvenation. Super-simple, super-tasty and good for both body and soul.

cauliflower & squash
CURRY

2 tablespoons vegetable oil

2 red onions, sliced

4 garlic cloves, crushed

4-cm/1½-inch piece each of fresh ginger and turmeric, peeled and grated

4 cardamom pods, bruised

1 lemongrass stalk, bruised

2 bird's eye chillies/chiles, halved

2 teaspoons garam masala

1 teaspoon ground cumin

500 g/1 lb. 2 oz. butternut squash, peeled, deseeded and cut into 1-cm/½-inch cubes

4 mini cauliflowers or 500 g/1 lb. 2 oz. cauliflower, cut into florets

2 sprigs of curry leaves

400-g/14-oz. can chickpeas, drained and rinsed

400-g/14-oz. can chopped tomatoes

400-ml/14-fl oz. can coconut milk

10 g/½ cup coriander/cilantro, leaves picked

freshly squeezed juice of ½ lime, plus extra wedges to serve

sea salt and freshly ground black pepper

brown rice and/or vegan naan breads, to serve

Place the oil and sliced onions in a wide, deep saucepan and cook over a gentle heat, with the lid on, for 5 minutes, stirring occasionally.

Add the garlic, ginger, turmeric, cardamom pods, lemongrass, chillies/chiles, garam masala and cumin, plus a splash of water to stop the pan from going dry, and cook the paste for about a minute.

Add the chopped butternut squash and mini cauliflowers or cauliflower florets, plus the curry leaves, chickpeas and canned tomatoes. Add the coconut milk and a little salt and pepper. Stir everything together and bring to the boil, then turn down the heat and cover with a lid.

Cook for 20–25 minutes until the vegetables are cooked through and the sauce has thickened. Add a splash more water if the pan gets too dry.

Add the coriander/cilantro and lime juice and serve with cooked brown rice and/or vegan naan breads and lime wedges, to squeeze over.

SERVES 4

CROWD-PLEASERS

This is a Greek-style vegetable bake that is delicious freshly made and warm, but even better the next day served at room temperature. Here, sweet potatoes are used, which pair beautifully with the other flavours.

CAULIFLOWER BRIAM

Preheat the oven to 220°C (425°F) Gas 7.

Add the olive oil, sweet potatoes, cherry tomatoes, courgettes/zucchini, aubergine/eggplant, onion, garlic, cauliflower and passata/strained tomatoes to a large bowl. Sprinkle with the oregano. Season generously with salt and pepper. Combine well with your hands and transfer to a large ovenproof dish. Drizzle with extra oil, if needed.

Bake in the preheated oven for 30 minutes, then turn the oven temperature down to 200°C (400°F) Gas 6. Bake for another 20–30 minutes, or until the top has browned and the vegetables are tender; add a little water if the dish gets too dry. Let cool slightly before serving.

SERVES 6

50 ml/3½ tablespoons extra-virgin olive oil, plus extra if needed

200 g/7 oz. sweet potatoes, scrubbed and skins left on, sliced into rounds

12 cherry tomatoes

3 courgettes/zucchini, sliced into rounds

1 large aubergine/eggplant, sliced into rounds

1 large onion, sliced into rounds

3 garlic cloves, crushed

250 g/9 oz. sprouting cauliflower or normal cauliflower

300 g/10½ oz. passata/strained tomatoes

30 g/1 oz. fresh oregano, leaves picked

sea salt and freshly ground black pepper

Who doesn't love a cosy night in with a warming curry to share amongst friends? This makes a fabulous and reasonably inexpensive supper for anyone following a plant-based diet, and is a great introduction to vegan cooking for those who don't. Serve the curry with chapatis and mango chutney – and vegan coconut yoghurt.

chickpea & almond
CURRY

2 onions, sliced

4–5 tablespoons olive oil

2 teaspoons garam masala

1 teaspoon ground turmeric

1 teaspoon ground coriander

1 teaspoon ground cumin

1 teaspoon chilli flakes/hot red pepper flakes

60 g/2¼ oz. fresh ginger

2 garlic cloves, finely chopped

2 x 400-g/14-oz. cans chopped tomatoes

2 x 400-g/14-oz. cans chickpeas, drained and rinsed

2 tablespoons good-quality tomato ketchup

80 g/¾ cup ground almonds

chopped fresh coriander/cilantro leaves

1 red chilli/chile, deseeded and sliced, to garnish

Preheat the oven to 190°C (375°F) Gas 5. Scatter the onion slices over the base of a deep sheet pan and drizzle with the olive oil. Add the garam masala, turmeric, ground coriander, cumin and chilli flakes/hot red pepper flakes. Stir to coat the onions in the spices. Roast for 10 minutes.

Peel the ginger and cut it into julienne. Remove the pan from the oven and add the ginger and chopped garlic. Stir in the chopped tomatoes, chickpeas, tomato ketchup and ground almonds. Return the pan to the oven and cook for about 20–25 minutes, until the sauce is lovely and thickened. Garnish with chopped coriander/cilantro and red chilli/chile slices.

SERVES 4

SERVES
4–6

Moussaka is not usually a meat-free dish, but here is a vegan version that's equally moreish.

LENTIL MOUSSAKA

In a pan, add 750 ml/3 cups water, the lentils, kombu and bay leaf, and bring to the boil, uncovered. Half-cover and simmer over a medium heat for 15 minutes. Add 110 ml/½ cup more cold water. Simmer for 20 minutes. Add a final 110 ml/½ cup cold water, increase the heat and cook for 20 minutes more. The lentils should have a texture like thick mash. Slice the kombu thinly and return it to the lentils. Discard the bay leaf.

Meanwhile, place the aubergine/eggplant slices in a large bowl with ½ teaspoon of the salt. Massage it in and let sit for at least 15 minutes. Pat dry with kitchen paper/paper towels. Prepare the potatoes and pat those dry as well.

Heat 1 tablespoon oil in a large frying pan/skillet and heat over a medium heat. Add half of the aubergine/eggplant, wait until the flesh starts browning, then turn. Repeat with the remaining slices. Add the rest of the oil to the pan and fry the potato slices in 3 batches, until golden on both sides. Then season with the remaining ½ teaspoon salt.

Preheat the oven to 180°C (350°F) Gas 4. Cover the bottom of the baking pan with fried potato slices. Spread over half of the lentils. Layer the aubergine/eggplant and spread over the tomato sauce, then add another layer of aubergine, and some potatoes, if any left. Cover with the remaining lentils.

To prepare the béchamel sauce, place the oil in a small pan, add the flour and beat for a couple of minutes over a medium heat until golden brown. Add the milk little by little, stirring continuously until the sauce boils and becomes creamy and thick, without any lumps. Add the white miso (if using), salt, nutmeg and pepper to taste. Beat once more, then pour over the lentils, spreading it evenly with a spatula. Bake for about 40 minutes, until well browned.

For the lentil layer

300 g/1½ cups dried brown lentils, washed and drained

6-cm/2½-inch strip of kombu seaweed

1 bay leaf

For the potato & aubergine/ eggplant layer

2 large aubergines/eggplants, cut lengthways into 3-mm/⅛-inch slices

1 teaspoon sea salt

650 g/1 lb. 7 oz. medium potatoes, cut into 2-mm/¹⁄₁₆-inch slices

100 ml/½ cup sunflower oil, for frying

350 ml/1½ cups good-quality tomato ketchup

For the béchamel

50 ml/3½ tablespoons olive oil

4 tablespoons millet flour or unbleached plain/all-purpose flour

580 ml/2½ cups soya/soy milk

1 tablespoon white miso (optional)

1 teaspoon sea salt

a pinch of ground nutmeg

freshly ground black pepper

a 23 x 30-cm/ 9 x 12-inch baking pan, well-oiled

Vegan pizza with hummus? Hell, yeah! The soft dough makes a perfect pizza crust, or pittas for lunch the next day!

HUMMUS PIZZA

For the dough

80 ml/⅓ cup lukewarm water

2 teaspoons maple sugar

9 g/1 tablespoon active dry yeast

400 g/3¼ cup plain/all-purpose flour, plus extra for dusting

100 g/¾ cup wholemeal/whole-wheat flour

1½ teaspoons sea salt

270 ml/1 cup plus 2 tablespoons lukewarm water

2 tablespoons olive oil, plus extra for oiling

For the topping

300 g/1½ cups Basic Hummus (see page 59)

1 onion, cut into half-moons

8 green olives, stoned/pitted

2 garlic cloves, thinly sliced

80 g/1 cup button mushrooms, very thinly sliced

1 teaspoon dried oregano

2 handfuls of rocket/arugula, to serve

8 cherry tomatoes, cut in half, to serve

olive oil, to serve

Beat together the water, maple sugar and yeast, and let rest, covered with a damp towel, in the oven with the light on for 30 minutes or until bubbly.

In a large bowl, beat together the flours and salt. Add the lukewarm water and oil, and mix in with a wooden spoon. Knead the dough in the bowl and then on a clean surface for 10 minutes. Don't add extra flour, the dough will be sticky but will come together eventually. Oil the bowl and the dough, place the dough in the bowl, cover with a damp towel and let rise in the oven with the oven light on for 3 hours or until doubled in size.

Preheat the oven to 250°C (475°F) Gas 9 and choose the 'lower heat element' setting, if possible. Divide the dough into two balls (approx. 200 g/7 oz. each) and place them on a floured surface. Let rise for another 10 minutes.

Flour two sheets of baking parchment and gently roll each ball into a 24-cm/9½-inch circle. Slide each one carefully onto a baking sheet. Spread 150 g/¾ cup hummus on top of each rolled-out pizza base. Top with onion, olives, garlic and mushrooms, and sprinkle over ½ teaspoon of dried oregano.

Carefully slide the baking parchment with one pizza directly onto the bottom of the oven, without the baking sheet. Bake for 5 minutes. Change the oven setting to 'top grill/broiler', if possible, open the oven, slide the pizza and parchment back onto the baking sheet and place in the upper part of the oven, so that the oven grill/broiler can crisp the toppings. Bake for 2–3 minutes. Take out and repeat with the other pizza. Top with rocket/arugula, tomatoes and a drizzle of oil, and serve.

MAKES 2 X
24-CM/9½-INCH
DIAMETER PIZZAS

Delicately flavoured with fragrant spices, this pretty rice dish is an excellent hearty meal on its own, or as an accompaniment to a larger vegan main.

TOMATO ALMOND
pilaff

Heat the margarine in a heavy-bottomed saucepan or pot set over a medium heat. Add the shallot, cinnamon stick and cardamom pods, and fry gently, stirring now and then, for 2 minutes, until the shallot softens.

Mix in the basmati rice, coating well with the margarine, then the tomato purée/paste. Pour over 300 ml/1¼ cups of water and season with salt. Bring the mixture to the boil, reduce the heat, cover and simmer for 10–15 minutes, until the water has all been absorbed and the rice is tender.

Meanwhile, scald the tomatoes. Pour boiling water over the tomatoes in a small pan or pot set over a medium heat. Heat for 1 minute, then remove from the water and carefully peel off the skin using a sharp knife. Halve the tomatoes, scoop out the soft pulp and finely dice the tomato shells.

When the rice is cooked, transfer to a serving dish or bowl. Fold in the diced tomatoes, sprinkle with the flaked/slivered almonds and coriander/cilantro, and serve at once.

25 g/1½ tablespoons vegan margarine

1 shallot, finely chopped

1 cinnamon stick

2 cardamom pods

200 g/1 cup basmati rice, rinsed

1 tablespoon tomato purée/paste

a pinch of sea salt

225 g/8 oz. tomatoes

25 g/3 tablespoons flaked/slivered almonds, dry-fried until golden

chopped fresh coriander/cilantro, to garnish

SERVES 4

These burgers make a great meaty alternative. They are deliciously savoury and just spicy enough, with wonderful sweet hints from the sun-dried tomatoes. The polenta/cornmeal gives the burger a lovely hint of crunch.

CHILLI VEGGIE BURGER
with sun-dried tomatoes

1 sweet potato

3 garlic cloves, skins on

olive oil, for drizzling

40 g/3 tablespoons green lentils

1 teaspoon vegetable bouillon powder

60 g/½ cup fresh wholemeal/whole-wheat breadcrumbs

1 carrot, grated

6–8 sun-dried tomatoes, finely chopped

1 medium–hot red chilli/chile, deseeded and finely chopped

1 teaspoon balsamic vinegar

1 teaspoon dried oregano

1 teaspoon dark soy sauce

1 teaspoon Cajun spice blend

2 tablespoons of ground flaxseeds/linseeds, mixed with 6 tablespoons of water

1 tablespoon plain/all-purpose flour

1 tablespoon polenta/cornmeal

celery salt and freshly ground black pepper

To serve

8 burger buns, warmed

rocket/arugula leaves

red onion chutney or relish

Preheat the oven to 160°C (325°F) Gas 3.

Peel the sweet potato and chop into 2.5-cm/1-inch cubes. Put in a roasting dish with the garlic and drizzle liberally with olive oil. Roast in the preheated oven for about 40 minutes, or until the potato is soft and just beginning to colour around the edges. Remove from the oven and let cool slightly.

Meanwhile, place the lentils in a pan of cold water with the vegetable bouillon, bring to the boil, then reduce the heat to a simmer and cook for 20–25 minutes until tender. Once the lentils are ready, drain them and place in a large mixing bowl.

To the lentils, add the breadcrumbs, carrot, sun-dried tomatoes, chilli/chile, vinegar, oregano, soy sauce and Cajun spice blend. Add the cooled sweet potato. Make sure the garlic is cool too, then squeeze it out from its skin into the mix too. Using your hands, thoroughly combine all the ingredients together. Season with celery salt and pepper. Add the flaxseed/linseed water mixture to the mix to bind everything together – again it is easiest to use your hands to do this. If the burger mix is too wet, add another handful of breadcrumbs to it.

Mix the flour and polenta/cornmeal together in a shallow bowl. Form the burger mix into 8 equal balls, roll in the flour and polenta/cornmeal mix and shape the ball into a burger shape. Cover with clingfilm/plastic wrap until ready to cook.

Heat a little olive oil in a frying pan/skillet and fry the burgers over a medium heat for 5 minutes each side, turning frequently. Serve in warm buns with rocket/arugula and red onion relish.

This recipe really shows how tasty and tempting vegan cheese can be – it's hard to resist the melted cheese in a comforting casserole-style dish!

heat-&-eat
FALAFEL CASSEROLE

Start by making the tomato sauce. Heat the olive oil in a pan over medium heat and sauté the onion until softened. Add the bouillon powder/cube, herbs, syrup and tamari, and stir until the onion soaks up the spices; about 2 minutes.

Add the passata/strained tomatoes and bring to the boil. Lower the heat and leave to simmer, uncovered,for about 10 minutes, or until thick. At the very end of cooking, add the garlic, parsley or chives and an extra drizzle of olive oil. Season to taste. This sauce can be made a couple of days in advance and kept refrigerated, if needed.

To assemble the casserole, preheat the oven to 180°C (350°F) Gas 4.

Drizzle a little olive oil in the bottom of the baking dish, pour in the tomato sauce, add a layer of falafel and then cover with the grated/shredded vegan cheese. Bake for 10–15 minutes, until the tomato sauce starts sizzling and the cheese melts. Serve with blanched broccoli or any other greens, toasted sourdough bread or creamy mashed potatoes.

Tip You can use store-bought falafel for this recipe, or use any leftovers from the falafel recipe on page 71.

230 ml/1 cup tomato sauce (see below)

7–9 falafel

50 g/½ cup grated/shredded white Cheddar-style vegan cheese

olive oil, to drizzle

blanched broccoli, toasted sourdough or creamy mashed potatoes, to serve

For the tomato sauce

3 tablespoons olive oil

1 large onion (about 120 g/4 oz.), finely chopped

1 teaspoon vegetable bouillon powder or ½ bouillon cube

1 teaspoon dried oregano or basil

1 tablespoon rice, agave or pure maple syrup

1 tablespoon tamari or soy sauce

230 ml/1 cup tomato passata/strained tomatoes

2 garlic cloves, crushed

2 tablespoons chopped fresh parsley or snipped chives

sea salt and freshly ground black pepper, to taste

a large baking dish

SERVES 2–3

Fajitas seem like the best party food to serve to a crowd, and here you have everything in one pan. Making up your own fajita whilst sat around the table with friends or family is such a sociable way to enjoy a meal, and everyone can take what they want to create their perfect fajita combination!

BAKED FAJITAS

2 medium sweet potatoes, peeled and chopped into 1.5-cm/½-inch pieces

3 teaspoons olive oil

2 (bell) peppers, deseeded and cut into 2-cm/¾-inch long slices

2 red onions, sliced into thin wedges

28-g/1-oz. package of fajita seasoning mix

400-g/14-oz. can chickpeas

To serve

Lighter Guacamole (see page 19)

coconut yoghurt

wraps or cooked rice

SERVES 4

Preheat the oven to 200°C (400°F) Gas 6.

Put the sweet potatoes on a large sheet pan that has sides. Drizzle over ½ teaspoon of the olive oil and bake in the preheated oven for 15 minutes.

Meanwhile, mix the (bell) peppers, onions, remaining 2½ teaspoons olive oil and the fajita seasoning together in a bowl.

Once the sweet potatoes have been baking for 15 minutes, add the (bell) pepper and onion mix to the sheet pan and stir. Bake for another 15 minutes.

Meanwhile, drain and rinse the chickpeas and add to the pan to cook for the last minute.

Serve with guacamole, coconut yoghurt and either wraps or rice, or both!

This Turkish dish is neither expensive nor over-indulgent in its use of oil. Nevertheless, it's still worth using good-quality extra-virgin olive oil.

stewed AROMATIC AUBERGINES

To prepare the aubergines/eggplants, keep the stalks on and peel off 4–5 vertical 2-cm/¾-inch strips of skin, from top to bottom, leaving a space between each peel so you are left with strips of skin and exposed flesh. Make a vertical cut right through the centre, from top to bottom, but leave both ends intact, so it holds together. Sprinkle salt over the exposed areas of flesh and inside the cut, and leave in a colander with a weighted plate on top to drain out some of the bitter juices.

Meanwhile make the filling. In a frying pan/skillet, gently sauté the onions with a little oil over a medium heat until soft. Take care not to colour them. Add in the garlic, coconut palm sugar and smoked/Spanish paprika and cook for another 2 minutes, without burning the garlic. Stir in the tomatoes and parsley. Season with salt and pepper, then remove from the heat.

Rinse the salt off the aubergines/eggplants and pat dry. Lay them in a medium pot that will fit them snugly, and divide the tomato mixture between them, carefully stuffing it into the incisions so as not to pull the 2 halves apart. Cover with the extra-virgin olive oil, lemon juice and enough water to submerge about ¾ of the aubergines/eggplants. Add in a good pinch of salt and pepper and place on a medium-high heat. Once bubbling, reduce the heat to low and leave to simmer for 1 hour with the lid on, until the aubergines/eggplants are completely soft. You may need to turn them half way through. Season to taste then let cool.

Serve at room temperature with the extra parsley sprinkled over and bread to mop up the liquid. This dish is even better the following day, so it is a great one to make in advance.

3 medium aubergines/eggplants

2 onions, about 245 g/½ lb., thinly sliced

1 tablespoon olive oil

5 garlic cloves, crushed

2 teaspoons coconut palm sugar

1 teaspoon smoked/Spanish paprika

300 g/10 oz. baby plum or cherry tomatoes, finely chopped

a large handful of chopped fresh flat-leaf parsley, plus extra to garnish

100 ml/scant ½ cup extra-virgin olive oil

freshly squeezed juice of ½ lemon

sea salt and freshly ground black pepper

crusty bread, to serve

SERVES 3–4

Stir-fries are a quick and easy go-to comfort food. The texture and flavour is great and you can use any coloured vegetables you like to make it look really appetizing.

VEGETABLE STIR-FRY

1 red and 1 green (bell) pepper, sliced into strips

3 carrots, cut into ribbons

150 g/5 oz. green French beans, sliced

100 g/3½ oz. baby corn, roughly chopped

2 pak choi/bok choy, sliced lengthways

coconut oil, for frying (optional)

black sesame seeds, to garnish

sesame oil, to drizzle

For the stir-fry sauce

½–1 teaspoon freshly grated ginger, to taste

½–1 green chilli/chile, thinly sliced, to taste

½ red chilli/chile, thinly sliced

1 garlic clove, finely chopped

a small handful of jarred pea aubergines/eggplants, roughly chopped (optional)

2 tablespoons pomegranate molasses

2 tablespoons liquid coconut aminos or soy sauce

freshly squeezed juice of 1 lime

First prepare the stir-fry sauce. Mix all the ingredients together in a small bowl and set aside until ready to cook.

The hard work in this dish is in the slicing of the vegetables. Prepare the ingredients as indicated, ensuring everything is sliced or chopped in a similar way to allow the ingredients to cook at the same time.

Set a large wok or frying pan/skillet over a high heat and add a little coconut oil or water. Add the vegetables and cook for about 1–2 minutes until you have the desired crunch.

Tip half of the stir-fry sauce into the pan and toss to coat. Continue to cook for 1–2 minutes longer to release the flavours of the sauce into the dish, then remove the pan from the heat.

Top the dish with black sesame seeds and drizzle with a little sesame oil. Serve immediately with the remaining stir-fry sauce on the side to pour over to taste.

SERVES 4

This stew is a vegan version of the dish 'succotash', which comes from m'sick-quotash, the Native American word for a mixture of sweetcorn and butter/lima beans, and many other vegetables, as well different types of meat.

BEAN, CORN & SQUASH
stew

Preheat the oven to 200°C (400°F) Gas 6.

In a large bowl, toss the squash cubes in 2 tablespoons of the oil, season with salt and pepper and add the whole sage leaves. Transfer to a baking sheet and roast in the preheated oven for 45–60 minutes, until the squash cubes are soft and the edges are beginning to brown. Set aside.

Meanwhile, in a large frying pan/skillet, heat the remaining oil with the margarine and fry the onion over a gentle heat until soft. Stir in the corn, the rest of the sage, the oregano and chilli/chile, then add the beans and a little water. Heat gently and simmer, covered, for 5 minutes. Add the roast squash (discard the sage, which will be charred), grate/shred the flesh of the tomatoes into the stew (discard the skin) and season to taste.

Cover the pan and heat everything through, then stir in the cream. Sprinkle with chopped chives or parsley and serve.

1 small butternut squash, peeled, deseeded and cut into bite-size chunks

3 tablespoons sunflower oil

10 fresh sage leaves, 5 whole and 5 shredded

30 g/2 tablespoons vegan margarine

1 onion, chopped

kernels from 2 corn cobs, scraped off with a sharp knife, or 250 g/1½ cups drained, canned or frozen sweetcorn

2 teaspoons dried oregano

1 red chilli/chile, deseeded and chopped (optional)

400-g/14-oz. can butter/lima beans, drained

3 tomatoes, halved horizontally

3 tablespoons vegan double/heavy or coconut cream

sea salt and freshly ground black pepper

chopped/snipped fresh chives or flat-leaf parsley, to garnish

KEEP IT SWEET

This is a frozen, chocolatey nut butter concoction, perfect for when you're craving chocolate. Pop one of these frozen treats in your mouth straight from the freezer and you'll be satisfied with a hit of pure cocoa. If you can find raw cocoa powder, use it in this recipe as its potency is greater than that of regular cocoa powder.

cocoa–almond
FREEZER FUDGE POPS

Put all the ingredients in a food processor or blender and blend until smooth.

Divide the mixture into 8 and roll each portion into a ball between the palms of your hands. Dust in cocoa powder.

Put the fudge pops onto a sheet pan or in an airtight container and freeze them for at least 30 minutes before eating. Store in the freezer for up to 4 weeks.

70 ml/¼ cup almond butter (or make your own, see page 16)

2 teaspoons ground flaxseeds/linseeds

1 large teaspoon coconut oil

1 large teaspoon sugar

1½ tablespoons unsweetened cocoa powder (preferably raw), plus extra for dusting

½ teaspoon pure vanilla extract

1 teaspoon espresso powder (optional)

MAKES 8

This recipe is one for a committed ice cream- or sorbet-maker. In Italian, frutti di bosco is translated as 'fruits from the forest' and is fabulous in combination with a lemon sorbet or creamy vegan gelato.

MIXED BERRY SORBET

In a saucepan set over a medium heat, gently heat 160 ml/²⁄₃ cup of the spring water until it reaches boiling point. Remove from the heat, add the lemon juice and stir in the sugar until it dissolves. Let the syrup cool for 30 minutes.

Put the berries and the remaining water in a food processor and blitz to a purée. Add the cooled syrup and blend briefly again until thoroughly mixed.

Pour the mixture into the ice cream maker and churn freeze according to the manufacturer's instructions.

The sorbet is best served immediately or can be kept in the freezer for up to 3–4 days.

360 ml/1½ cups spring water

freshly squeezed juice of ½ lemon

160 g/¾ cup plus 1 tablespoon caster/superfine sugar

500 g/1 lb. 2 oz. ripe organic berries, such as raspberries, strawberries (stalks removed), blackberries and blueberries

an ice cream maker

SERVES 4

Take five ingredients and blitz yourself a raw, vegan chocolate brownie – a healthy way to satisfy any sweet tooth!

BROWNIE SQUARES

Put all the ingredients in a food processor and blitz until they are well combined and you have a smooth and rather sticky paste. If it is too dry, add 2 or more tablespoons of agave or maple syrup.

Scrape the mixture into the prepared baking pan and smooth level with your hands. If you don't have the correct size of pan, lay a sheet of clingfilm/plastic wrap on a board, scrape the mixture onto the sheet and shape it with your hands into a rough rectangle about 2.5 cm/1 inch thick. Wrap in clingfilm/plastic wrap.

Refrigerate for 1 hour before cutting into 6 squares to serve.

300 g/2½ cups cashew nuts

120 g/generous ¾ cup walnuts

110 g/1 cup raw cacao powder

100 g/⅔ cup soft, pitted dates

1 tablespoon coconut oil, agave or pure maple syrup, to taste (optional)

a deep, 22 x 15-cm/ 8¾ x 6-inch baking pan or container, lined with baking parchment (optional)

MAKES 6 LARGE PORTIONS

Not only are these muffins vegan, they're also gluten-free.
If you like, you can make a sliceable loaf cake — simply
bake the mixture in a loaf pan lined with baking parchment
for 35 minutes at the same oven temperature.

blueberry heaven
YOGHURT BERRY MUFFINS

70 g/½ cup potato starch

1 teaspoon bicarbonate of soda/baking soda

1 teaspoon baking powder

1 teaspoon xanthan gum

60 g/½ cup brown rice flour

60 g/½ cup teff flour

3 tablespoons milled flaxseeds/linseeds

125 g/½ cup coconut yoghurt

2 tablespoons of ground flaxseeds/linseeds mixed with 6 tablespoons of water

70 ml/⅓ cup vegetable oil

70 ml/⅓ cup pure maple syrup or agave syrup

180 ml/¾ cup apple or pear purée

1 teaspoon pure vanilla extract

a large handful of blueberries

a muffin pan, lined with baking parchment or paper cases

Preheat the oven to 180°C (350°F) Gas 4.

Sift the potato starch, bicarbonate of soda/baking soda, baking powder and xanthan gum into a mixing bowl. Add in the remaining dry ingredients then beat the wet ingredients into the mix one at a time, before folding in the blueberries.

You can also substitute the apple or pear purée for store-bought fruit flavoured baby food.

Spoon the muffin mixture into the prepared muffin pan. Bake for 17 minutes or until cooked through and golden brown on top.

Serve immediately or store in an airtight container for an any-time-of-day treat.

MAKES ABOUT 10 MUFFINS

Coffee drinker or not, these treats are irresistible, and the icing adds a sweet kick for your taste buds!

coffee toffee
COOKIES

Preheat the oven to 180°C (350°F) Gas 4.

If using cocoa beans, grind them in a coffee or spice grinder to a fine powder.

Beat together the oil, sugar, milk, coffee extract and vinegar. In a separate bowl, sift together the flour and baking powder, then stir in the flaxseeds/linseeds, vanilla powder, ground almonds, salt and cinnamon. Tip into the bowl of wet ingredients and mix into a smooth dough with a spatula.

Divide the dough into 25 and roll into balls. Arrange them on the prepared baking sheets about 2 cm/¾ inch apart. Gently flatten each ball with the back of a spoon, trying to avoid making cracks. Bake in the preheated oven for 9–10 minutes – they should still be a little soft. Let cool completely on the baking sheets.

For the icing, it's better to finely grind the sugar in a coffee or spice grinder, but you can also try without grinding it. Mix the cornflour/cornstarch into the milk in a heatproof bowl. Add the coffee extract and sugar and mix. Set over a saucepan of simmering water (do not let the base of the bowl touch the water) and beat well for a couple of minutes to allow the starch to thicken slightly over the steam. Remove from the heat, then let cool for 10 minutes.

Spoon some icing over each cookie, then sprinkle over some chopped nuts. Allow to set for at least 1 hour after which the icing shouldn't be sticky, but smooth and firm to the touch.

Store for up to 2 weeks in an airtight container at room temperature, or, in the summer months, in the fridge.

30 g/⅓ cup raw cocoa beans (or nibs) or 30 g/⅓ cup unsweetened cocoa powder

100 g/½ cup coconut oil

100 g/½ cup Demerara sugar

60 ml/¼ cup soya/soy milk

2 teaspoons coffee extract

¼ teaspoon apple cider vinegar

200 g/1½ cups spelt flour

½ teaspoon baking powder

1 tablespoon ground flaxseeds/linseeds

¼ teaspoon bourbon vanilla powder (or pure vanilla extract)

2 tablespoons ground almonds

¼ teaspoon sea salt

¼ teaspoon ground cinnamon

chopped nuts, for sprinkling

For the icing

65 g/⅓ cup Demerara sugar

1 tablespoon cornflour/cornstarch

2 tablespoons soya/soy milk

1 teaspoon coffee extract

baking sheets, lined with baking parchment

A good doughnut can evade even accomplished bakers, and that's because everyone knows what the perfect one should taste like – airy, moist and soft, these will hit the spot!

MINI BAKED DOUGHNUTS
with cinnamon 'sugar'

For the doughnuts

160 g/1⅓ cups plain/all-purpose flour

½ teaspoon xanthan gum

65 g/⅓ cup sugar

1½ teaspoons baking powder

1 teaspoon bicarbonate of/baking soda

1 teaspoon ground cinnamon

½ teaspoon sea salt

125 ml/½ cup almond or rice milk (or make your own, see page 15)

2 tablespoons apple cider vinegar

1½ tablespoons sunflower oil

5 tablespoons unsweetened apple purée/applesauce

1 teaspoon pure vanilla extract

For the cinnamon 'sugar'

1 big serving spoon vegan margarine (about 60 ml/¼ cup, but it doesn't need to be precise)

2 teaspoons ground cinnamon

5 tablespoons sugar

1-2 mini-doughnut pans (enough to make 24 doughnuts), greased with coconut oil

a disposable piping bag fitted with a plain nozzle/tip

Preheat the oven to 180°C (350°F) Gas 4.

For the doughnuts, put the flour, xanthan gum, sugar, baking powder, bicarbonate of/baking soda, cinnamon and salt in a large bowl. Stir with a balloon/wire whisk.

Put the milk and vinegar in a small bowl; you will see a kind of 'buttermilk' start to form after a couple of minutes. Once this happens, add the sunflower oil, apple purée/applesauce and vanilla extract. Pour the wet mixture into the bowl of dry ingredients and you should see some bubbles form – this is what will make the doughnuts nice and fluffy! Use the whisk again to stir really gently, and stop as soon as the mixtures have combined.

Fill a piping bag with the mixture and pipe the mixture into the holes of the doughnut pan(s). Bake in the preheated oven for 5–6 minutes and keep an eye on them – they are so small that they bake very quickly.

Meanwhile, make the cinnamon sugar. Melt the margarine and put in a bowl. Separately, combine the cinnamon and sugar. Remove the baked doughnuts from the pan(s) and dip the top of each one into the melted margarine, then straight into the cinnamon sugar. Serve immediately – they taste best when straight from the oven, but they will also keep for about 2 days in an airtight container.

Using rice milk and coconut milk and cream for this gooey rice 'pudding' will put any dairy-free doubters at bay. For the toppings, feel free to get creative and use whatever combination you like. Medjool dates and nut butter swirled though the rice is another must-try.

COCONUT RICE PUDDING
with blueberries & syrup

Rinse the rice thoroughly under running water and add to a pot with the coconut milk and rice milk and bring to the boil. Reduce the heat to low and simmer gently for about 20–35 minutes, stirring regularly to ensure the rice does not stick to the bottom. By this stage the rice should be cooked through with a thick and creamy consistency. Stir in the vanilla extract, cinnamon, nutmeg, salt and maple syrup and taste, adding a little more of anything you particularly like.

When ready to serve, ladle the hot rice into bowls and add in a few frozen blueberries (or whatever topping you choose), straight from the freezer. Drizzle over a little maple syrup and serve immediately. The blueberries will thaw out in the hot pudding, leaving gorgeous inky pools of juice as you eat.

150 g/¾ cup risotto rice, carnaroli or arborio

400-ml/14-fl. oz. can coconut milk

600 ml/2½ cups rice or almond milk (or make your own, see page 15)

1 teaspoon pure vanilla extract

½ teaspoon ground cinnamon

a good pinch of grated nutmeg, about ¼ teaspoon

a pinch of sea salt

3 tablespoons pure maple syrup, plus extra to drizzle over

a handful of frozen blueberries

SERVES 4

Warming and full of sticky-sweet fruit, this dessert is lovely to serve on a stormy evening when everyone feels shivery and miserable — this is sure to raise a smile!

PEACH CRUMBLE

8 firm but ripe peaches

2–3 tablespoons apple juice concentrate

1 tablespoon plain/all-purpose flour

a pinch of sea salt

dairy-free vanilla custard, to serve

For the crumble

80 g/⅔ cup hazelnuts or other nuts

65 g/½ cup plain/all-purpose flour

50 g/½ cup rolled/old-fashioned oats

grated zest of 1 orange or lemon

¼ teaspoon ground cinnamon

⅛ teaspoon bourbon vanilla powder or pure vanilla extract

a pinch of sea salt

85 g/⅓ cup agave syrup

50 g/⅓ cup vegan margarine

a deep ovenproof dish

Preheat the oven to 150°C (300°F) Gas 2.

For the crumble, put the nuts in a baking pan and roast them in the preheated oven for 8–10 minutes. Rub off any skins that have loosened from the nuts, then roughly chop the nuts by hand or in a food processor or blender. Big pieces will burn while the crumble is baking, so make them quite small.

Put the flour, oats, zest, cinnamon, vanilla powder or extract and salt in a bowl and stir. Add the syrup and mix well, then work the margarine in with your hands, rubbing it between your fingers. When the mixture becomes crumbly, add the chopped nuts.

Preheat the oven to 180°C (350°F) Gas 4.

Blanch the peaches in a saucepan of boiling water for 1–2 minutes – just long enough to be able to peel the skin off easily. Transfer them to a bowl of cold water so you don't burn your fingers, then peel off the skin. Halve and stone/pit the peaches and cut them into wedges. Toss them with the apple juice concentrate, flour and salt. Spread them in the ovenproof dish, then cover them evenly with the crumble.

Bake in the preheated oven for about 35 minutes or until the crumble topping is golden brown and the juice is bubbling up around the edges.

The crumble is best served warm with dairy-free vanilla custard, but if you happen to have leftovers and serve it as a dessert the next day, I'm sure no one will complain!

SERVES 6–8

SERVES 8–10

Chocolate and orange is a great flavour combination when it comes to desserts. This pie looks elaborate but it's deceptively simple to make and delicious to eat.

CHOCOLATE ORANGE PIE

In a food processor, pulse all the base ingredients together until they form a thick paste. Scoop out the mixture and press it into the bottom of the cake pan. Put in the freezer to set.

Next, prepare the filling. Rinse your food processor and blend all of the ingredients together until completely smooth. Pour on top of your base and freeze again for at least 2 hours, to set.

Remove the pie from the freezer 20 minutes before serving. Sprinkle with extra orange zest to garnish and enjoy.

This pie will keep for up to 2 weeks in the freezer, and 3 days in the fridge, once thawed.

For the base

500–650 g/4–5 cups almonds

60 g/½ cup dried unsweetened figs

3 tablespoons cacao nibs

1 tablespoon coconut oil

½ teaspoon pure vanilla extract

For the filling

155 g/1¼ cups pine nuts, soaked overnight

½ tablespoon grated orange zest, plus extra to garnish

125 ml/½ cup freshly squeezed orange juice

90 g/¾ cup raw cacao powder

60 ml/¼ cup coconut oil

5 tablespoons granulated sugar (or up to 8 tablespoons for extra sweetness)

a 23-cm/9-inch round springform cake pan, greased and lined with baking parchment

INDEX

RECIPE CREDITS

Nadia Arumugan
Buddha's Delight

Jordan Bourke
Coconut Rice Pudding
Stewed Aromatic Aubergines

Chloe Coker & Jane Montgomery
Home-made Baked Beans
Vegetable Tagine

Amy Ruth Finegold
Buckwheat & Flaxseed
 Pancakes
Chocolate Almond Butter
 Smoothie
Coconut Breakfast Cookies
Blueberry Heaven Yoghurt
 Muffins
Pumpkin Pie Oatmeal

Liz Franklin
Chickpea & Almond Curry

Nicola Graimes
Make-Your-Own Nut Milks
Marinated Mushroom, Crispy
 Kale & Rice Salad
Popeye Special

Dunja Gulin
Basic Hummus
Cashew 'Yoghurt' Sauce
Cherry Tomatoes filled with
 Spinach Pesto
Chickpea Flour & Harissa
 Patties
Coffee Toffee Cookies
Fried Tofu Sandwiches
Ginger, Peas & Tahini Pasta
Heat-&-Eat Falafel
 Casserole
Hummus Pizza
Lentil Moussaka
Preparing Tofu, Seitan &
 Tempeh
Peach Crumble
Red Lentil Falafel Wraps
Simple & Filling Chia Seed
 Porridge
Tofu Mayonnaise
Tofu Scramble

Vicky Jones
Bean, Corn & Squash Stew
Chickpea Fritters

Kathy Kordalis
Cauliflower Briam
Cauliflower & Squash Curry

Anya Ladra
Beet Pâté
Brownie Squares

Jenny Linford
Potato Straws
Tomato Almond Pilaf
Tomato, Freekeh & Avocado
 Salad

Dan May
Chilli Veggie Burgers
Fruity African Bean Stew

Hannah Miles
Carrot & Ginger Soup with
 Pickled Carrot Baguettes
Salt & Pepper Popcorn
Three Bean Chilli Baked
 Potato

Adriano di Petrillo
Mixed Berry Sorbet

Louise Pickford
'Pick-Me-Up' Power Bowl

Rosa Rigby
Cinnamon 'Granola' with
 Pear & Cranberry Compote
Vegetable Stir-Fry

Shelagh Ryan
Smashed Avo on Toast with
 Raw Courgettes & Dukkah

Jenny Tschiesche
Baked Fajitas
Cumin-Roasted Chickpeas

Leah Vanderveldt
Roasted Aubergine Po' Boys

Laura Washburn Hutton
Ancho-Roasted Squash
 Tacos
Apple Coleslaw
Noodles with Sesame-
 Peanut Sauce

Jenna Zoe
Almond-Crusted Buffalo Bites
Aubergine 'Bacon' Sandwich

Chocolate Orange Pie
Cocoa-almond Freezer
 Fudge Pops
Jalapeño Onion Rings
Lighter Guacamole
Mini Baked Doughnuts with
 Cinnamon 'Sugar'
Nut & Seed Butters
Spicy Tomato Kale Chips
Zesty Almond Pesto

PHOTOGRAPHY CREDITS

Ed Anderson Page 76

Tim Atkins Pages 21, 68, 69, 70, 114

Peter Cassidy Pages 6, 12, 22, 82, 86, 110, 113

Laura Edwards Page 125

Tara Fisher Pages 53, 118, 136

Richard Jung Page 93

Mowie Kay Pages 1, 36, 37, 58, 101, 109, 121

Adrian Lawrence Pages 78, 79, 81

William Lingwood Pages 64, 65, 128, 129

Steve Painter Pages 2, 25, 85, 89, 105, 117, 127

William Reavell Pages 26, 27, 38, 39, 44, 48, 49, 60, 61, 62, 72, 73, 98, 99, 106, 116, 120, 122, 123

Matt Russell Page 97

Kate Whitaker Pages 5, 7, 14, 24, 31, 90, 91, 126, 144

Isobel Wield Page 77

Claire Winfield Pages 17, 18, 28, 30, 35, 40, 42, 43, 47, 50, 54, 57, 66, 67, 74, 94, 124, 130, 131, 132, 133, 135, 138, 139, 140, 141